THE MOST AGONIZING CRY

Eli, Eli, Lama Sabachthani?

Barry S Ross

THE MOST AGONIZING CRY

BY

BARRY S. ROSS

DEDICATION

I DEDICATE THIS BOOK TO GOD ALMIGHTY FOR HIS DIVINE
INSPIRATION OF IT INTO THE SPIRIT OF MY MIND. I
DEDICATE TO YOU THE READER IN THE HOPE THAT IT WILL
INSPIRE YOU TO CONTINUE TO GROW IN THE GRACE AND IN
THE KNOWLEDGE OF OUR LORD AND SAVIOR JESUS CHRIST.

ELI, ELI, LAMA SABACHTHANI?

Barry S Ross

CONTENTS

ACKNOWLEDGMENTS

First and far most I acknowledge God Almighty for it is by his mercy and grace that you and I are blessed with this awesome gift of faith and live and walk by the same. It is God that work within the spirit of our minds to both will [have the desire] and to do [power to carry out the desire] of his good pleasures. I also acknowledge my Publishers [createspace/amazon] for their wonderful work in the publication of all my God inspired works. You are an awesome blessing to all self-published authors. And last but certainly not least to you the reader. Thank you for your purchase of this book and it is my sincerest prayer that it be an awesomely inspired tool to help edify your faith.

CHAPTER ONE
THE CRY OF DEATH

As the Spirit of Almighty God is inspiring the spirit of my mind to write this book entitled, The Most Agonizing Cry: subtitled, Eli, Eli, Lama Sabachthani: which is, being interpreted, My God, my God, why hast thou forsaken me?

The most agonizing cry in the words thereof continues to ring throughout this present evil world of which you and I today live! It is indeed, the most agonizing cry ever heard in any individual's death.

This very second in time, I myself, am shivering on the inside of the spirit of my very being! A most devastating and horrible cry: My God, my God, WHY hast thou forsaken me?

This same identical cry is heard within the pages of scripture, wherein the death of Christ Jesus is told in detail by those disciples that is documented within scripture, were eyewitnesses of this most horrifying, most unjust legalized murder ever committed. Listen to the death cry of Christ Jesus, our Lord, our savior, and our GOD in the moments of his final breath of life as is documented by Matthew according to **(Matthew-27:45-50 KJV:)**

1

"... Now from the sixth hour there was darkness over all the land until the ninth hour. And about the ninth hour Jesus cried with a loud voice, saying, Eli, Eli, lama Sabachthani?" that is to say, My God, my God why hast thou forsaken me? Some of them that stood there, when they heard that, said, This man calleth for Elias. And straightway one of them ran, and took a spunge, and filled it with vinegar, and put it on a reed, and gave him to drink. The rest said, Let be, let us see whether Elias will come to save him. Jesus, when he had cried again with a loud voice, yielded up the ghost...."

That my friend, is the most agonizing cry which cry is heard around this world, to the generation that should not pass away until all be fulfilled.

Help me Holy Ghost: My friend, Christ Jesus cried again, with a loud voice, and as is document in the above documentation, gave up the ghost: Some biblical translations read gave up his spirit: Others renders; and then he died: Others renders, his Spirit departed: however the rendering form any biblical translation have it rendered, the one which drives the mental picture, if, you will, home to within the spirit of my own mind is the GOD'S WORD TRANSLATION (GWT) wherein it be rendered as follows: **"... Then Jesus loudly cried out once again and gave up his life...."**

Looking again at the details of the above documentation of Matthew's gospel as seen through the eyes of Matthew the words of Christ Jesus with his final breath were Eli, Eli, Lama Sabachthani? That is to say, My God, my God, why hast thou forsaken me? I wish I had SOMEBODY that is in the Spirit with me: SOMEBODY, that knows where GOD is taking us with this thing: Hello here somebody! God is taking us within the spirit of our mind a little bit higher within the pages of this book:

Watch this now or you will miss it: Somewhere in another place within the sacred scriptures it is therein documented regarding to the death of Christ Jesus these words:
"... And he made his grave with the wicked, and with the rich in his death; because he had done no violence, neither was any deceit in his mouth. Yet it pleased the LORD to bruise him; he hath put him to grief: when thou shalt make his SOUL an offering for sin, he shall see his seed, he shall prolong his days, and the pleasure of the LORD shall prosper in his hand. He shall see of the travail of his SOUL, and shall be satisfied: ...
[Watch this now or you will miss it: The Merriam-Webster Dictionary defines the word TRAVAIL as follows: (1:) painful work or exertion: toil (2:) Agony, torment. In other words my friend, the TRAVAIL of the SOUL of Christ Jesus was and yet remains within 'the most agonizing cry!' Wherein Jesus cried with a loud voice a second time out to God the Father; Eli, Eli, Lama Sabachthani? That is to say, My God, my God, why hast thou forsaken me? It is vital and very significant that you comprehend within the spirit of your mind this biblical fact and truth: that being this; The rendering of biblical translations of the word spirit in all reality of my personal studies references "the SOUL" wherein is LIFE (physical life and its consciousness) which be located within the human anatomy – THE BLOOD!

Please note with me in the pages of YOUR own BIBLE **(Leveticus-17:11)** these words of documentation: **"... For the life of the flesh is in the blood: and I have given it unto you upon the altar to make an atonement for your SOULS: for it is the BLOOD that maketh atonement for the soul...."**

Therefore, in essence, the LIFE or the SOUL of Christ Jesus was IN HIS BLOOD!

Therein IS the BREATH of LIFE or Spirit essence if you will. I heard someone SUM it all up like this: OUR SPIRIT IS GOD'S BREATH. OUR LIFE IS HIS GIFT. God breathes LIFE into DEAD things at HIS will – watch this if you will or you will miss it: Looking back at **(Genesis-2:7 KJV)** this biblical truth is therein documented:
"… And the Lord God formed man of the dust of the ground, and breathed into his nostrils the breath of life; and man became a living SOUL…." [Yes, that is correct my friend, the man scripture called Adam was as DEAD as dead could be after he was formed of the dust of the ground and he remained in that state of being (Lifeless) until GOD breathed the BREATH of LIFE into the nostrils of the man Adam, at which time something supernatural took place: The man BECAME a living SOUL!] I can hear within the spirit of my mind the Spirit of God reminding me of the inspired words of the prophet Isaiah as we pick up this thought of the details of the death of Christ Jesus where we left off according to **(Isaiah-53:11-12 KJV)** continuing it is documented as follows:
… by his knowledge shall my righteous servant justify many; for he shall bear their iniquities. Therefore will I divide him a portion with the great, and he shall divide the spoil with the strong; BECAUSE he hath poured out his SOUL unto death: …

Watch this or you will miss it: Christ Jesus at his death poured out his precious BLOOD wherein was his very SOUL unto DEATH! Christ Jesus died that you and I might live. Only blood God said can atone for the soul. In times of old prior to the coming of Christ Jesus, Almighty God allowed for animals without spot or blemish to make an atonement for the souls of the Israelites. Christ Jesus was the end of animal sacrifices offered up to God by priest who's blood is tainted with sin: But Jesus's BLOOD is even today untainted with sin! Precious is the blood of the Lamb of God that came into this evil world to die for the sins of humanity! Scripture declares that yet while we ourselves were sinners Christ Jesus died for us. God himself was IN Christ reconciling the world unto himself! It was for that declaration of which Christ proclaimed and that he and his Father were one in the same and that when they saw him they saw the Father: It was for these declarations Christ Jesus was accused of blasphemy and it was for that very accusation the Jews crucified the Son of the living God, Christ Jesus!

"... I and my Father are one. Then the Jews took up stones again to stone him. Jesus answered them, Many good works have I shewed you from my Father; for which of those works do you stone me? The Jews answered him, saying, For a good work we stone thee not; but for blasphemy; and because that thou, being a man, makest thyself God...." (John-10:30-33 KJV).

Watch this now or you will miss it: The prophet Isaiah ultimately declared these vital words being inspired of God regarding the death of Christ Jesus as I lift up out of Isaiah chapter fifty-three the second half of the twelfth verse and it is therein documented by the prophet Isaiah:

... and he was numbered with the transgressors; and he bare the sins of many, and made intercession for the transgressors."

The transgressors include you and me prior to being saved of God through Christ Jesus our sacrificial Lamb without spot or blemish. Come quickly due to my lack of time as Almighty God leads me within the spirit of my mind to the book of Hebrews and therein note with me if you will **(Hebrews-5:1-10 KJV)** wherein the apostle Paul was inspired of God to document these very significant words:

"For every high priest taken from among men is ordained for men in things pertaining to God, that he

may offer both gifts and sacrifices for sins: Who can have compassion on the ignorant, and on them that are out of the way; for that he himself also is compassed with infirmity. And by reason hereof he ought, as for the people, so also for himself, to offer for sins. And no man taketh this honour unto himself, but he that is called of God, as was Aaron. So also Christ glorified not himself to be made an high priest; but he that said unto him, Thou art my Son, today have I begotten thee. As he saith also in another place, Thou art a priest for ever after the order of Melchisedec. Who in the days of his flesh, when he had offered up prayers and supplications with strong crying and tears unto him that was able to save him from death, and was heard in that he feared; Though he were a Son, yet learned he obedience by the things which he suffered; And being made perfect, he became the author of eternal salvation unto all them that obey him; Called of God a high priest after the order of Melchisedec...."

"... Forasmuch then as the children are partakers of flesh and blood, he also himself likewise took part of the same; that through death he might destroy him that had the power of death, that is, the devil; And deliver them who through fear of death were all their lifetime subject to bondage. For verily he took not on him the nature of angels; but he took on him the seed of Abraham. Wherefore in all things it behooved him to be made like unto his brethren, that he might be a merciful and faithful high priest in all things pertaining to God, to make reconciliation for the sins of the people. For in that he himself hath suffered being tempted, he is able to succor them that are tempted." (Hebrews-2:14-18 KJV). The apostle writes in Hebrews chapter one these words:

"God, who at sundry times and in divers manners spake in time past unto the fathers by the prophets, Hast in these last days spoken unto us by his Son, whom he hath appointed heir of all things, by whom also he made the worlds; Who being the brightness of his glory, and thee express image of his person, and upholding all things by the word of his power, when he had by himself purged our sins, sat down on the right hand of the majesty on high; Being made so much better than the angels, as he hath by inheritance obtained a more excellent name then they...."

Watch this now or you will miss it: In another place the apostle Luke, the beloved physician was inspired of God to write these inspiring words of truth regarding the apostles Peter and John upon the healing of a lame beggar regarding this more excellent name then the angels:

"... Then Peter, filled with the Holy Ghost said unto them, Ye rulers of the people, and elders of Israel, If we this day be examined of the good deed done to the impotent man, by what means he is made whole; Be it known unto you all, and to all the people of Israel, that by the name of JESUS CHRIST of Nazareth, whom ye crucified, whom God raised from the dead, even by him doth this man stand here before you whole. This is the stone which was set at nought of you builders, which is become the head of the corner. Neither is there salvation in any other: [Watch this now somebody or you will miss it] For there is none other NAME under heaven given among men, whereby we MUST be saved...." (Acts-4:8-12 KJV).

Yes, my friend, Christ Jesus died for you and for me while you and I was yet sinners! He was our sacrificial Lamb of God. He was indeed the promised prophet liken unto Moses! Christ Jesus died not only for the sins of believers says the word of Almighty God, but, for the sins of the world or humanity if you will.

Oh, my God, but that most agonizing cry! The cry that have rocked the very foundations of this earth. The cry that was so agonizing that it moved even God the Father: It was a most horrific cry of all times:

"... Eli, Eli, Lama Sabachthani? that is, My God, my God, why hast thou forsaken me? ..."

Yes, my friend, that cry have resonated down through time even to our time since the death of Christ Jesus on the cross at Calvary!

It is the cry of death with the last breath of Christ Jesus! Scripture declares that Melchisedec who in the days of his flesh, when he had offered up prayers and supplications with strong crying and tears unto him that was able to save him from death, and was heard in that he feared; Though he were a Son, yet learned he obedience by the things which he suffered;

The prophet Isaiah declared according to **(Isaiah-53:10-11 KJV)** these very inspired words as we lift them out of that chapter once more for the sake of stirring up the spirit of our minds:

"...Yet it pleased the LORD to bruise him; he hath put him to grief: when thou shalt make his soul an offering for sin, he shall see his seed, he shall prolong his days, and the pleasure of the LORD shall prosper in his hand. He shall see of the travail of his soul, and shall be satisfied: by his knowledge shall my righteous servant justify many; for he shall bare their iniquity...."

You my friend, are reading The Most Agonizing Cry; Eli, Eli, Lama Sabachthani?

CHAPTER TWO
ELI, ELI, LAMA SABACHTHANI?

"...He shall see of the TRAVAIL of his soul, and shall be satisfied: ..." the prophet Isaiah was inspired of Almighty God to write in Isaiah chapter fifty-three lifting up the first half of verse eleven.

The prophet in the above verse is making reference to Christ Jesus' sacrificial work of his life or his soul. This work of salvation would be the most horrific work in human histroy. Christ Jesus would have to suffer, shed his precious blood and die, for the sins of humanity: He would give his life a ransom for many.

Christ Jesus as is documented in the gospel of John according to **(John-12:23-26 KJV)** predicted his death and the process that he would have to lay down his life and die that many might live; he explained it as follows:

"...And there were certain Greeks among them that came up to worship at the feast: The same came therefore to Philip, which was of Bethsaida of Galilee, and desired him, saying, Sir, we would see Jesus. Philip cometh and telleth Andrew: and again Andrew and Philip tell Jesus. And Jesus answered them, saying, The hour is come, that the Son of man should be glorified.

Verily, verily, I say unto you, Except a corn of wheat fall into the ground and die, it abideth alone: but if it die, it bringeth forth much fruit. He that loveth his life shall lose it; and he that hateth his life in this world shall keep it unto life eternal. If any man serve me, let him follow me; and where I am, there shall also my servant be: if any man serve me, him will my Father honour. Now is my soul troubled; and what shall I say? Father, save me from this hour: but for this cause came I unto this hour. Father, glorify thy name. Then came there a voice from heaven, saying, I have both glorified it, and will glorify it again. The people therefore, that stood by, and heard it, said that it thundered: others said, An angel spake to him. Jesus answered and said, This voice came not because of me, but for your sakes. Now is the judgment of this world: Now shall the prince of this world be cast out. ...

Watch this now or you will miss it: In the apostle John's revelation given him by Christ Jesus on the Isle of Patamas according to that which John documented in **(Revelation-12:7-12 KJV)** as it be written:

"...**And there was war in heaven: Michael and his angels fought against the dragon; and the dragon fought and his angels, And prevailed not; neither was their place found anymore in heaven. And the great dragon was cast out, that old serpent, called the Devil, and Satan, which deceiveth the whole world: he was cast out into the earth, and his angels were cast out with him. And I heard a loud voice saying in heaven, Now is come salvation, and strength, and the kingdom of our God, and the power of his Christ: for the accuser of our brethren is cast down, which accused them before our God day and night. And they overcame him by the BLOOD of the LAMB, and by the word of their** testimony; and they loved not their lives unto the death. Therefore rejoice, ye heavens, and ye that dwell in them. Woe to the inhabiters of the earth and of the sea! for the devil is come down unto you, having great wrath, because he knoweth that he hath but a short time. And when the dragon saw that he was cast down unto the earth, he persecuted the woman which brought forth the man child. And to the woman was given two wings of a great eagle, that she might fly into the wilderness, into her place, where she is nourished for a time, and times, and half a time, from the face of the serpent. And the serpent cast out of his mouth water as a flood after the woman, that he might cause her to be carried away of the flood. And the earth helped the woman, and the earth opened her mouth, and swallowed up the flood which the dragon cast out of his mouth. And the dragon was wroth with the woman, and went to make war with the remnant of her seed, which keep the commandments of God, and have the testimony of Jesus Christ."

After the voice which came from heaven, which voice the people heard, Christ Jesus, declared to them that NOW is the JUDGMENT of this world: Now shall the prince of this world be cast out. Watch this now or you will miss it; then Christ Jesus continued as I began to lift up **(John-12:32 continuing)**

...And I, If I be lifted up from the earth will draw all men unto me. This he said signifying what death he should die. The people answered him, We have heard out of the law that Christ abideth for ever: and how sayest thou, The Son of man must be lifted up? who is this Son of man? Then Jesus said unto them, Yet a little while is the light with you. Walk while ye have the light, lest darkness come upon you: for he that walketh in

darkness knoweth not whither he goeth. While ye have light, believe in the light, that ye may be the children of light. These things spake Jesus, and departed, and did hide himself from them. But though he had done so many miracles before them, yet they believed not on him: That the saying of Esaias the prophet might be fulfilled, which he spake, Lord, who hath believed our report? and to whom hath the arm of the Lord been revealed?... These things said Esaias, when he saw his glory, and spake of him...."

Jesus said to the disciples and to the people, The hour is come, that the Son of man should be glorified. Christ Jesus also said that, Now is my soul troubled; and what shall I say, Father save me from this hour: but for this cause came I into this hour.

Christ Jesus knew that his soul or his physical life and its consciousness was going to be poured out shortly and he was going to have to shed his BLOOD to save a dying world filled with every sort of evil act imaginable. His hour had come: There was a spiritual war taking place in heaven among the angels of God and the angels of the Devil, which war, the Devil and his angels lost and were cast down into this earth!

God can have no parts of sin. GOD can have NO parts of sin. God cannot have any parts of sin!

It is for THIS cause the Spirit of Almighty God departed from Christ Jesus at the very split second at his death; when he took on the sins of the world – all of humanity included! Jesus on the cross, mutilated, humiliated, depleted, emptying or pouring out his very soul unto death, CRYED the most AGONIZING cry any human being ever heard in human history! It was a cry which broke the heart of his own mother Mary as she stood at the foot of his cross: A cry which devastated the disciple whom Jesus loved: It was a cry unto his very demise: It my friend was the most agonizing cry. Lord have mercy on us all as indeed it is our sins and our iniquities for which Christ Jesus died!

Christ Jesus spoke of Isaiah the prophet's words being fulfilled through the scriptures: Let me take you in the spirit of your mind back to the words documented by Isaiah when Isaiah saw the Lord's glory!

"Who hath believed our report? and to whom is the arm of the LORD revealed? For he shall grow up before him as a tender plant, and as a root out of a dry ground: he hath no form nor comeliness; and when we shall see him, there is no beauty that we should desire him. He is despised and rejected of men; a man of sorrows, and acquainted with grief: and we hid as it were our faces from him; he was despised, and we esteemed him not. Surely he hath borne our griefs, and carried our sorrows: yet we did esteem him stricken, smitten of God, and afflicted. But he was wounded for our transgressions, he was bruised for our iniquities: the chastisement of our peace was upon him; and with his stripes WE are healed. All we like sheep have gone astray; we have turned everyone to his own way; and the LORD hath laid on him the iniquity of us all. He was oppressed, and he was afflicted, yet he opened not his mouth: he is brought as a lamb to the slaughter, and as a sheep before her shearers is dumb, so he openeth not his mouth. He was taken from prison and from judgment: and who shall declare his generation? for he was cut off out of the land of the living: for the transgressions of my people was he stricken. And he made his grave with the wicked, and with the rich in his death; because he had done no violence, neither was any deceit in his mouth. Yet it pleased the LORD to bruise him; he hath put him to grief: when thou shalt

make his soul an offering for sin, he shall see his seed, he shall prolong his days, and the pleasure of the LORD shall prosper in his hand. He shall see of the travail of his soul, and shall be satisfied: by his knowledge shall my righteous servant justify many; for he shall bare their iniquities. Therefore will I divide him a portion with the great, and he shall divide the spoil with the strong; because he hath poured out his SOUL unto death: and he was numbered with the transgressors; and he bare the sin of many, and made intercession for the transgressors." (Isaiah-53:1-12 KJV.)

The most agonizing cry which cry was unto death: It was a death cry of separation from God the Father: It was so horrific that it caused God to move nature itself by the power of his mighty hand: Watch this my friend or you will miss it:

"...Now from the sixth hour there was darkness over all the land unto the ninth hour. And about the ninth hour Jesus cried with a loud voice, saying, Eli, Eli, Lama Sabachthani? that is to say, My God, my God, why hast thou forsaken me? ...Jesus when he had cried again with a loud voice, yielded up the ghost. And, behold, the veil of the temple was rent in twain from the top to the bottom; and the earth did quake, and the rocks rent; And the graves were opened; and many bodies of the saints which slept arose, And came out of their graves after his resurrection, and went into the holy city, and appeared unto many. Now when the centurion, and they that were with him, watching Jesus, saw the earthquake, and those things that were done, they feared greatly, saying, Truly this WAS the SON of GOD. ..." (Matthew-27:45,46,50-54KJV.)

CHAPTER THREE
FROM BIRTH TO DEATH

"Now the birth of Jesus Christ was upon this wise: When his mother Mary was espoused to Joseph, before they came together, she was found with child of the Holy Ghost. Then Joseph her husband, being a just man, and not willing to make her a publick example, was minded to put her away privily. But while he thought on these things, behold, the angel of the Lord appeared unto him in a dream, saying, Joseph, thou son of David, fear not to take unto thee Mary thy wife: for that which is conceived in her is of the Holy Ghost. And she shall bring forth a son, and thou shalt call his name JESUS: for he shall save his people from their sins:... [Watch this now or you will miss it as God is taking us somewhere here] The apostle John documents these vital words concerning this Christ Jesus:

"... For God so loved the world, that he gave his only begotten Son, that whosoever believeth in him should not perish but have everlasting life. For God sent not his Son into the world to condemn the world; but that the world through him might be saved. He that believeth on him is not condemned.... [Watch this now or you will miss it] **"There is therefore now no condemnation to them which are in Christ Jesus, who walk not after the flesh, but after the Spirit. For the law of the Spirit of life in Christ Jesus hath made me free from the law of sin and death. For what the law could not do, in that it was weak through the flesh, God sending his own Son in the likeness of sinful flesh, and for sin, condemned sin in the flesh: That the righteousness of the law might be fulfilled in us, who walk not after the flesh, but after the Spirit. For they that are after the flesh do mind the things of the flesh: but they that are after the Spirit the things of the Spirit. For to be carnally minded is death; but to be spiritually minded is life and peace. Because the carnal mind is enmity against God: for it is not subject to the law of God, neither indeed can be. So then they that are in the flesh cannot please God. But ye are not in the flesh, but in the Spirit, if so be that the Spirit of God dwell in you. Now if any man have not the Spirit of Christ, he is none of his. And if Christ be in you, the body is dead because of sin; but the Spirit is life because of righteousness. But if the Spirit of him that raised up Jesus from the dead dwell in you, he that raised up Christ from the dead shall also quicken your mortal bodies by his Spirit that dwelleth in you. Therefore, brethren, we are debtors, not to the flesh, to live after the flesh. For if ye live after the flesh, ye shall die: but if you through the Spirit do mortify the deeds of the body, ye shall live. For as many that are led by the Spirit of God, they are the sons of God. For ye have not received the spirit of bondage again to fear; but ye have received the Spirit of adoption, whereby we cry, Abba, Father. The Spirit itself bear witness with our spirit, that we are the children of God: And if children, then heirs; heirs of**

God, and joint-heirs with Christ; if so be that we suffer with him, that we may be also glorified together...." **(Romans-8:1-17 KJV.)**

God is taking us some place so let us follow the Spirit of the Almighty God in this thing known as the birth of Jesus Christ, and of God so loving this world that he gave his only begotten Son, not to condemn the world but that the world through his Son might be saved – looking again at (John-3:18-19, 36 KJV) wherein John documents the continuality of the details:

... but he that believeth not is condemned already, because he hath not believed in the name of the only begotten Son of God. And this is the condemnation, that light is come into the world, and men loved darkness rather than light, because their deeds were evil.... He that believeth on the Son hath everlasting life: and he that believeth not the Son shall not see life; but the wrath of God abideth on him."

Apostle Paul the final disciple that saw the glorified Christ on the road to Damascus, as of one born out of due time declared these significant words according to that which be documented in **(Hebrews-10:1-10 KJV:)**
"For the law having a shadow of good things to come, and not the very image of the things, can never with those sacrifices which they offered year by year continually make the comers thereunto perfect. For then would they not have ceased to be offered? because that the worshippers once purged should have had no more conscience of sins. But in those sacrifices there is a remembrance again made of sins every year. For it is not possible that the blood of bulls and of goats should take away sins. Wherefore when he cometh into the world, he saith, Sacrifice and offering thou wouldest not, but a body hast thou prepared me. In burnt

offerings and sacrifices for sin thou hast had no pleasure. Then said I, Lo, I come (in the volume of the book it is written of me,) to do thy will, O God. Above when he said, Sacrifice and offering and burnt offerings and offering for sins thou wouldest not, neither hath pleasure therein, which are offered by the law; then said he, Lo, I come to do thy will, O God. He taketh away the first, that he may establish the second. By the which will we are sanctified through the offering of the body of Jesus Christ once for all. And every priest standeth daily ministering and offering oftentimes the same sacrifices, which can never take away sins: But this man, after he had offered one sacrifice for sins for ever, sat down on the right hand of God; from henceforth expecting till his enemies be made his footstool. For by one offering he hath perfected for ever them that are sanctified. Whereof the Holy Ghost also is a witness to us: for after that he had said before, This is the covenant that I will make with them after those days, saith the Lord, I will put my laws into their hearts, and in their minds will I write them; And their sins and iniquities will I remember no more. Now where remission of these is, there is no more offering for sin.

Watch this now or you will miss it as we take a journey into the spirit of the mind of the apostle John as John was in the Spirit on the Lord's day or the day of the Lord; wherein the apostle documents what he saw of those that believed not in their lifetimes in the name of the only begotten Son of God and whom the bible says, if they did not believe were condemned already!

"… And I saw a great white throne, and him that sat on it, from whose face the earth and the heaven fled away; and there was found no place for them. And I saw the dead, small and great, stand before God; and the books were opened: and another book was opened, which is the book of life: and the dead were judged out of those things which were written in the books, according to their works. And the sea gave up the dead which were in it; and death and hell [the grave] delivered up the dead which were in them: and they were judged every man according to their works. And death and hell [the grave] were cast into the lake of fire.** [The bible's literal hell – the second death that is.] **This is the second death. And whosoever was not found written in the book of life was cast into the lake of fire." (Revelation-20:11-14 KJV.)

We, who believe in the name of the Son of God, at the split second of our deaths, will not, have to stand in this final judgment – believers are excluded. Thank God for Jesus, right? But let's take a look at what else the apostle declared he seen in the spirit of his mind in this vision projected into the future even past our time but very, very near the ending of all things:

"And I saw an angel come down from heaven, having the key of the bottomless pit and a great chain in his hand. And he laid hold on the dragon, that old serpent, which is the Devil, and Satan, and bound him a thousand years, And cast him into the bottomless pit, and shut him up, and set a seal upon him, that he should deceive the nations no more, till the thousand years should be fulfilled: and after that he must be loosed for a season. And I saw thrones, and they that sat on them, and judgment was given unto them: and I saw the souls of them that were beheaded for the witness of Jesus, and for the word of God, and which had not worshipped the beast, neither his image, neither had received his mark upon their foreheads, or in their hands; and they lived and reigned with Christ a thousand years. But the rest of the dead lived not again until the thousand years were finished. This is the first resurrection. Blessed and holy is he that hath part in the first resurrection: on such the second death hath no power, but they shall be priest of God and of Christ, and shall reign with him a thousand years. And when the thousand years are expired, Satan shall be loosed out of his prison, And shall go out to deceive the nations which are in the four corners of the earth, Gog and Magog, to gather them together to battle: the number of whom is as the sand of the sea. And they went up upon the breadth of the earth, and compassed the camp of the saints about, and the beloved city: and fire came down from God out of heaven, and devoured them. And the devil that deceived them was cast into the lake of fire and brimstone, where the beast and the false prophet are, [Were is the correct translation,] and shall be tormented day and night for ever and ever...." (Revelation-20:1-10 KJV.)

In the prophet Daniel's vision of the ancient of days; Daniel testifies of the final judgment, and of the end of Satan, the devil, his demons and of the kingdom of God on the earth: Daniel documented these terrifying yet glorious details of the future that is close at hand before our very eyes: **"... I beheld until the thrones were cast down, and the Ancient of days did sit, whose garment was white as snow, and the hair of his head was like the pure wool: his throne was like the fiery flame, and his wheels as burning fire. A fiery stream** [I believe this fiery stream is the lake of fire – the second death] **issued and came forth from before him: thousand thousands ministered unto him, and ten thousand times ten thousand stood before him: the judgment was set, and the books were opened...." (Daniel-7:9-10 KJV.)** I believe this to be the very same vision that was shown to the apostle John except with deeper details. Watch this now or you will miss it as God takes us to another place of documentation in the scriptures:

In the closing of chapter three I discern the Spirit of God taking the spirit of my mind back into time, the time of another prophet named Joel as God want you to hear these words God inspired the spirit of the mind of Joel to proclaim to those that believe not in the name of the only begotten son of God, in that day, as the Almighty projected the spirit of the mind of Joel into the near future past the lifetime of Joel and even your and my time:

"… Proclaim ye this among the Gentiles; Prepare war, wake up the mighty men, let all the men of war draw near; let them come up: Beat your plowshares into swords, and your pruninghooks into spears: let the weak say I am strong. Assemble yourselves, and come, all ye heathen, and gather yourselves together round about: thither cause the mighty ones to come down, O LORD. Let the heathen be wakened, and come up to the valley of Jehoshaphat: for THERE will I sit to judge all the heather round about. Put ye in the sickle, for the harvest is right: come, get you down; for the press is full, the fats overflow; for their wickedness is great. Multitudes, multitudes in the valley of decision: [The valley of Armageddon.] **for the day of the LORD is near in the valley of decision. The sun and the moon shall be darkened, and the stars shall withdraw their shinning. The LORD also shall roar out of Zion, and utter his voice from Jerusalem; and the heavens and the earth shall shake:…" (Joel-3:9-16 KJV.)**

Almighty God have projected the spirit of the mind of Joel into a time [WORLD WAR III – nuclear, biological, and chemical warfare in this earth is for sure ahead of us] way beyond his own lifetime, even past yours and mine probably; into a day not too far off and God gave Joel this command: **"Blow ye the trumpet in Zion, and sound an alarm in my holy mountain: let all the inhabitants of the land tremble: for the day of the LORD cometh, for it is nigh at hand; A day of darkness and gloominess, a day of clouds and of thick darkness, as the morning spread upon the mountains: a great people and a strong; there hath not been ever the like, neither shall be anymore after it, even to the years of many generations...." (Joel-2:1-2 KJV.)**

Looking once again at the words of the apostle John as John declared that he that believeth not shall not see life and that the divine wrath of God abideth on him; That wrath will abide on into the afterlife even to the great white throne judgment. Remember this my friend:

"... He that believeth on the Son hath everlasting life; he that believeth not shall not see life, and the wrath of God abideth on him." (John-3:36 KJV.)

CHAPTER FOUR
A GLIMPSE INTO WORLD WAR III

The apostle John declared that at the first resurrection that the saints of God will reign with Christ for a thousand years at which time Satan – the dragon will be bound but that's not the end of John's vision, he sees in the Spirit what come AFTER the thousand years of Christ's and his heirs reign, the short time of Satan's release from his prison: watch this or you will miss it as all HELL breaks out in this earth when the fifth and sixth angels sound:

"And the fifth angel sounded, and I saw a star fall from heaven unto the earth: and to him was given the key of the bottomless pit. And he opened the bottomless pit; and there arose a smoke out of the pit, as the smoke of a great furnace; and the sun and the air were darkened by reason of the smoke of the pit. And there came out of the smoke locust upon the earth: and unto them was given power, as the scorpions of the earth have power. And it was commanded them, that they should not hurt the grass of the earth, neither any green thing, neither any tree; but only those men which have not the seal of God in their foreheads. And to them it was given that they should not kill them, but that they should be

tormented five months: and their torment was as the torment of a scorpion , when he striketh a man. And in those days shall men seek death, and shall not find it; and shall desire to die, and death shall flee from them. And the shapes of them were like unto horses prepared unto battle; and on their heads were as it were crowns of Gold, and their faces were as the faces of men. And they had hair as the hair of women, and their teeth were as the teeth of lions. And they had breastplates, as it were breastplates of iron; and the sound of their wings was as the sound of chariots of many horses running to battle. And they had tails like unto scorpions, and their stings were in their tails: and their power was to hurt men five months. And they had a king over them, which is the angel of the bottomless pit, whose name in the Hebrew tongue is Abaddon, but in the Greek tongue hath his name Apollyon. One woe is past; and behold, there come two woes more hereafter. And the sixth angel sounded, and I heard a voice from the four horns of the golden altar which is before God, Saying to the sixth angel which had the trumpet, Loose the four angels which are bound in the great river Euphrates. And the four angels were loosed, which were prepared for an hour, and a day, and a month, and a year, for to slay the third part of men. And the number of the army of the horsemen were two hundred thousand thousand: and I heard the number of them. And thus I saw the horses in the vision, and them that sat on them, having breastplates of fire, and of jacinth, and brimstone: and the heads of the horses were as the heads of lions; and out of their mouths issued fire and smoke and brimstone. By these three was the third part of men killed, by the fire, and by the smoke, and by the brimstone, which issued out of their mouths. For their power is in their mouth, and in their tails: for their tails were like unto serpents, and had heads, and with them they do hurt. And the rest of the men that were not killed by these plagues yet repented not of the works of their hands, that they should not worship devils, and idols of gold, and silver, and brass, and stone, and of wood: which neither can see, nor hear, nor walk: Neither repented they of their murders, nor of their sorceries, nor of their fornication, nor of their thefts...."

The prophet or preacher Zechariah, also was projected into the day of the Lord in the spirit of his being or mind in his lifetime and he described that dreadful, dreadful day as such:

"Behold, the day of the LORD cometh, and thy spoil shall be divided in the midst of thee. For I will gather all nations against Jerusalem unto battle; and the city shall be taken, and the houses rifled, and the women ravished; and half of the city shall go forth into captivity, and the residue of the people shall not be cut off from the city. Then shall the LORD go forth, and fight against those nations, as when he fought in the day of battle. And his feet shall stand in that day upon the mount of Olives, which is before Jerusalem on the east, and the mount of Olives shall cleave in the midst thereof toward the east and towards the west, and there shall be a very great valley; and half of the mountain shall move towards the north, and half of it towards the south. And ye shall flee to the valley of the mountains; for the valley of the mountains shall reach unto Azal: yea, ye shall flee, like as ye fled from before the earthquake in the days of Uzziah king of Judah: and the LORD my God shall come, and all the SAINTS with thee. And it shall come to pass in that day, that the light shall not be clear, nor dark: But it shall be one day which shall be known to the **LORD,** not day, nor night: But it shall come to pass, that at even time it shall be light. And it shall be in that day, that living waters shall go out from Jerusalem, half of them toward the former sea, and half of them from the hinder sea: in summer and in winter shall it be. And the **LORD** shall be king over all the earth: In that day shall there be one **LORD,** and his name one. All the land shall be turned as a plain from Geba to Rimmon south of Jerusalm: and it shall be lifted up, and inhabited in her place, from Benjamin's gate unto the place of the first gate, unto the corner gate, and from the tower of Hananeel unto the king's winepresses. And men shall dwell in it, and there shall be no more utter destruction; but Jerusalem shall be safely inhabited. And this shall be the plague wherewith the **LORD** will smite all the people that have fought against Jerusalem; Their flesh shall consume away while they stand on their feet, and their eyes shall consume away in their holes, and their tongue shall consume away in their mouth. And it shall come to pass in that day, that a great tumult from the **LORD** shall be among them; and they shall lay hold every one on the hand of his neighbor, and his hand shall rise up against the hand of his neighbor...."

Come back in here John and sum all this up if you will by that which is documented according to **(Revelation-16:1-23 KJV ...)**
"And I heard a great voice out of the temple saying to the seven angels, Go your ways, and pour out the vials of the wrath of God upon the earth. And the first went, and poured out his vial upon the earth; and there fell a noisome and grievous sore upon the men which had the mark of the beast, and upon them which worshipped his image. And the second angel poured out his vial

upon the sea; and it became as the blood of a dead man: and every living soul died in the sea. And the third angel poured out his vial upon the rivers and fountains of waters; and they became blood. He waters say, Thou art righteous, O Lord, which art, and wast, and shalt be, because thou hast judged thus. For they have shed the blood of the saints and prophets, and thou hast given them blood to drink; for they are worthy. And I heard another out of the altar say, Even so, Lord God Almighty, true and righteous are thy judgments. And the fourth angel poured out his vial upon the sun; and power was given unto him to scorch men with fire. And men was scorched with great heat, and blasphemed the name of God, which hath power over these plagues: and they repented not to give him glory. And the fifth angel poured out his vial upon the seat of the beast; and his kingdom was full of darkness; and they gnawed their tongues for pain, And blasphemed the name of the God of heaven because of their pains, and their sores, and repented not of their deeds. And the sixth angel poured out his vial upon the great river Euphrates; and the waters thereof was dried up, that the way of the kings of the east might be prepared. And I saw three unclean spirits like frogs come out of the mouth of the dragon, and out of the mouth of the beast, and out of the mouth of the false prophet. For they are the spirits of devils, working miracles, which go forth unto the kings of the earth and of the whole world, to gather them to the battle of that great day of God Almighty. Behold, I come as a thief. Blessed is he that watcheth, and keepeth his garments, lest he walk naked, and they see his shame. And he gathered them together into a place called in the Hebrew tongue Armageddon. [To the valley of Jehoshaphat – the valley of decision where Almighty God will sit in judgment – a place called in the Hebrew tongue Armageddon.] **And the seventh angel poured out his vial into the air; and there came a great voice out of the temple of heaven, from the throne, saying, It is done. And there were voices, and thunders, and lightnings; and there was a great earthquake, such as was not since men was upon the earth, so mighty an earthquake, and so great. And the great city was divided into three parts, and the cities of the nations fell: and great Babylon came in remembrance before God, to give unto her the cup of the wine of the fierceness of his wrath. And every island fled away, and the mountains were not found. And there fell upon men a great hail out of heaven, every stone about the weight of a talent: and men blasphemed God because of the plague of the hail; for the plague thereof was exceeding great."**

"… And I saw another angel fly in the midst of heaven, having the everlasting gospel to preach unto them that dwell on the earth, and to every nation, and kindred, and tongue, and people, Saying with a loud voice, Fear God, , and give glory to him; for the hour of his judgment is come: and worship him that made heaven, and earth, and the sea, and the fountains of waters…."
(Revelation-14:6-7 KJV.)

Yes, my friend, that was the true Light that light every man that come into the world. He was in this world, and the world was made by him, and the world knew him not. He came to his own [the Jews] and his own received him not. But as many as received him, to them gave he power to become the sons of God, even to them [us] that believe on his name: Which were born not of blood, nor of the will of the flesh, nor of the will of man, but of God.

CHAPTER FIVE
THE LEGACY OF JESUS CHRIST

The legacy of our Lord, our Savior, and our God is summed up in three powerful, powerful verses of scripture, which verses be as follows; Watch this now or you will miss it:

"… And Jesus went about all Galilee, teaching in their synagogues, and preaching the gospel of the kingdom, and healing all manner of sickness and all manner of disease among the people. And his fame went throughout all Syria: and they brought unto him all sick people that were taken with divers diseases and torments, and those which were possessed with devils, and those which were lunatic, and those that had the palsy; and he healed them…. (Matthew-4:23-24 KJV.)

My friend you are reading The Most Agonizing Cry – Eli, Eli, Lama Sabachthani: that is to say, My God, my God, Why hast thou forsaken me?

"…I speak not of you all: I know whom I have chosen: but that the scripture may be fulfilled, He that eateth bread with me (John-13:18-30 KJV) hath lifted up his heel against me. Now I tell you before it come, that, when it is come to pass, ye may believe that I am he. Verily, verily I say unto you, He that receiveth

whomsoever I send receiveth me; and he that receiveth me receiveth him that sent me. When Jesus had thus said he was troubled in spirit, and testified, and said, Verily, verily, I say unto you, that one of you shall betray me. Then the disciples looked one on another, doubting of whom he spake. Now there was leaning on Jesus' bosom one of his disciples, whom Jesus loved. Simon Peter therefore beckoned to him, that he should ask who it should be of whom he spake. He then lying on Jesus' breast saith unto him, Lord, who is it? Jesus answered, He it is, to whom I shall give sop, when I have dipped it. And when he had dipped the sop, he gave it to Judas Iscariot, the son of Simon. And after the sop Satan entered him. Then said Jesus unto him, That thou doest, do quickly. Now no man at the table knew for what intent he spake this unto him. For some of them thought, because Judas had the bag, that Jesus had said unto him, Buy those things that we have need of against the feast; or, that he should give something to the poor. He then having received the sop went immediately out: and it was night...." [John's account.]

"... And when the hour was come, he sat down, and the twelve apostles with him. And he said unto them, With desire I have desired to eat this Passover with you before I suffer. For I say unto you, I will not any more eat thereof, until it be fulfilled in the kingdom of God. And he took the cup, and gave thanks, and said, Take this, and divide it among yourselves: For I say unto you, I will not drink of the fruit of the vine, until the kingdom of God shall come. And he took bread, and gave thanks, and break it, and gave unto them, saying, This is my body which is given for you. Likewise also the cup after supper, saying, This cup is the new testament in my blood, which is shed for you. But, behold, the hand of him that betrayeth me is with me on the table. And truly the Son of man goeth, as it was determined: but woe unto the man by whom he is betrayed! And they began to inquire among themselves, which of them it was that should do this thing...." [Luke's account (Luke-22:14-23 KJV).]

"... And as they did eat, Jesus took bread, and blessed, and brake it, and gave to them, and said, Take, eat: This is my body. And he took the cup, and when he had given thanks, he gave it to them: and they all drank of it. And he said unto them, This is my blood of the new testament, which is shed for many. Verily I say unto you, I will drink no more of the fruit of the vine, until that day that I drink it new in the kingdom of God. And when they had sung a hymn, they went out into the mount of Olives...." [Mark's account (Mark-14:22-26 KJV).]

"... Then one of the twelve, called Judas Iscariot, went unto the chief priests, And said unto them, What will ye give me, and I will deliver him unto you? And they covenanted with him for thirty pieces of silver. And from that time he sought opportunity to betray him. Now the first day of the feast of unleavened bread the disciples came to Jesus, saying unto him, Where wilt thou that we prepare for thee to eat the Passover? And he said, Go into the city to such a man, and say unto him, The Master saith, My time is at hand; I will keep the Passover at thy house with my disciples. And the disciples did as Jesus had appointed them; and they made ready the Passover. Now when the even was come, he sat down with the twelve. And as they did eat he said, Verily I say unto you, that one of you shall betray me. And they were exceeding sorrowful, and began every one of them to say unto him, Lord, is it I?

And he answered and said, , He that dippeth his hand with me in the dish, the same shall betray me. The Son of man goeth as it is written of him: but woe unto that man by whom the Son of man is betrayed! It had been good for that man if he had not been born. Then Judas, which betrayed him, answered and said, Master, is it I? He said unto him, Thou hast said. And as they were eating, Jesus took bread, and blessed it, and brake it, and gave it to the disciples, and said, take, eat; this is my body. And he took the cup, and gave thanks, and gave it to them, saying, Drink ye all of it; For this is my blood of the new testament, which is shed for many for the remission of sins. But I say unto you, I will not drink henceforth of this fruit of the vine, until that day when I drink it new with you in my Father's kingdom. And when they had sung an hymn, they went out into the mount of Olives.... [Matthew-26:14-30 KJV).]

Now let me take you deeper into this betrayal of Judas Iscariot as is told by Matthew: Jesus told the twelve disciples; Woe be unto the man by whom the Son of man is betrayed; It had been better for that man if he had not been born: Wow, that just sent chills up my spine – Judas Iscariot – the son of perdition is in serious, serious trouble with God for his betrayal of Jesus Christ: Watch this now or you will miss it: Come on Matthew, continue telling the story:

... Then said Jesus unto them, All ye shall be offended because of me "THIS" night: for it is written, I will smite the shepherd, and the sheep of the flock shall be scattered abroad. But after I am risen again, I will go before you into Galilee. Peter answered and said unto him, Though all men shall be offended because of thee, yet will I never be offended. Jesus said unto him, Verily, I say unto thee, That this night, before the cock crow, thou shalt deny me thrice. Peter said unto him, Though

I should die with thee, yet will I not deny thee. Likewise also said all the disciples. Then cometh Jesus with them unto a place called Gethsemane, and said unto the disciples, Sit ye here, while I go and pray yonder. And he took with him Peter, and the two sons of Zebedee, and began to be sorrowful and very heavy. Then said he unto them, My soul is exceeding sorrowful, even unto death: tarry ye here, and watch with me. And he went a little further, and fell on his face, and prayed, Saying, O Father, if it be possible, let this cup pass from me: nevertheless not as I will, but as you wilt. And he cometh unto the disciples, and findeth the asleep, and saith unto Peter, What, Could ye not watch with me one hour? Watch and pray, that ye enter not into temptation: the spirit indeed is willing, but the flesh is weak. He went away again the second time, and prayed, saying, O my Father, If this cup may not pass away from me, except I drink it, thy will be done. And he came and found the asleep again: for their eyes were heavy. And he left them, and went away again, and prayed the third time, saying the same words. Then cometh he to his disciples, and saith unto them, Sleep on now, and take your rest: behold, the hour is at hand, and the Son of man is betrayed into the hands of sinners. Rise, let us be going: behold, he is at hand that doth betray me. And while he yet spake, lo, Judas, one of the twelve, came, and with him a great multitude with swords and staves, from the chief priest and elders of the people. Now he that betrayed him gave them a sign, saying, Whomsoever I shall kiss, that same is he: hold him fast. And forthwith he came to Jesus, and said, Hail, master; and kissed him. And Jesus said unto him, Friend, wherefore art thou come? Then came they, and laid hands on Jesus, and took him. And, behold, one of them which were with Jesus stretched out his hand, and drew his sword, and struck a servant of the high priest's, and smote off his ear. Then said Jesus unto him, Put up again thy sword into his place: for all they that take the sword shall perish with the sword. Thinkest thou that I cannot now pray to my Father, and he shall presently give me more than twelve legions of angels? But how then can the scriptures be fulfilled, that thus it must be? In that same hour said Jesus to the multitudes, Are ye come out as against a thief with swords and staves for to take me? I sat daily with you teaching in the temple, and ye laid no hold on me. But all this was done that the scriptures of the prophets might be fulfilled. Then all the disciples forsook him, and fled. And they that had laid hold on Jesus led him away to Caiaphas the high priest, where the scribes and the elders were assembled. But Peter followed him afar off unto the high priest's palace, and went in, and sat with the servants, to see the end. Now the chief priests, and elders, and all the counsel, sought false witness against Jesus, to put him to death; But found none: yea, though many false witnesses came, yet found they none. At the last came two false witnesses, And said, This fellow said, I am able to destroy the temple of God, and to build it in three days. And the high priest arose, and said unto him, Answerest thou nothing? what is it which these witness against thee? But Jesus held his peace. And the high priest answered and said unto him, I adjure thee by the living God, that thou tells us whether thou be the Christ, the Son of God. Jesus saith unto him, Thou hast said: nevertheless I say unto you, Hereafter shall ye see the Son of man sitting on the right hand of power, and coming in the clouds of heaven. Then the high priest rent his clothes, saying, He hath spoken blasphemy; What further need have we of witnesses? behold, now we have heard his blasphemy. What think ye? They answered and said, He is guilty of death. Then did they spit in his face, and buffeted him; and others smote him with the palms of their hands. , Saying, Prophesy unto us, thou Christ, Who is he that smite thee? Now Peter sat without in the palace: and a damsel came unto him, Thou also wast with Jesus of Galilee. But he denied before them all, saying, I know not what thou sayest. And when he was gone out into the porch, another maid saw him, and said unto them that were there, This fellow also was with Jesus of Nazareth. And again he denied with an oath, I do not know the man. And after a while came unto him they that stood by, and said to Peter, Surely thou also art one of them; for thy speech bewrayeth thee. Then, begain he to curse and sware, saying, I know not the man. And immediately the cock crew. And Peter remembered the word of Jesus, which said unto him, Before the cock crow, thou shalt deny me thrice. And he went out and wept bitterly. (Matthew-26:31-75 KJV.)

As I reread the details of this documentation, it is so disturbing to the spirit of my mind of what Jesus endured just for my own personal sins, and yours, and not just yours and mine, but for the sins of the entire world. What details Matthew is giving us, while Matthew has been long deceased, yet the disciple and apostle still speak touching billions of souls worldwide today.

Judas Iscariot betrayed Jesus with what I call the kiss of death and for only thirty pieces of silver. Somebody said that Satan himself, not one of his demonic spirits – fallen angels, but Satan, the devil himself entered Judas. Satan took total, absolute, complete control of the spirit of the mind of Judas Iscariot, possessing the spirit of Judas' mind. We all need to be reminded of these details from time to time or as often as possible to keep the story fresh within the spirit of our minds. But through it all Jesus, Matthew said, didn't say a word in front of the Sanhedrin or his false accusers until the ending of his hearing.

The disciples had fled and deserted him, Peter we learn followed at a far distance to see what would become of Jesus. Peter denied Jesus with an oath and yes, cursing: the details of Matthew doesn't tell exactly what curse words Peter used and certainly it is no telling but we do know that Peter was afraid for his own physically life and he was certainly outraged! Peter was no joke when he became angry.

Peter denied knowing or being with Jesus three time and scripture says, after which the cock crew!
Matthew described the demeanor of Peter at the end going out of the palace weeping bitterly! Now Matthew continues with what took place the following morning, watch this or you will miss it:
"When the morning was come, all the chief priests and elders took counsel against Jesus to put him to death; and when they had bound him, they led him away, and delivered him to Pontius Pilate the governor. Then Judas, which had betrayed him, when he saw that he was condemned, repented himself, and brought again the thirty pieces of silver to the chief priests and elders, Saying, I have sinned in that I have betrayed innocent blood....
[Watch now or you will miss it, at what them devil inspired hypocrites said to him]
... And they said, What is that to us? see thou to that. And he cast down the pieces of silver in the temple, and departed, and went and hanged himself. And the chief priests took the silver pieces, and said, It is not lawful for to put them in the treasury, because it is the price of

blood. And they took counsel, and bought with them the potter's field, to bury strangers in. Wherefore that field was called, The field of blood, unto this day. Then was fulfilled that which was spoken by Jeremy the prophet, saying, And they took the thirty pieces of silver, the price of him that was valued, who they of the children of Israel did value; And gave them for the potter's field, as the Lord appointed me. And Jesus stood before the governor: and the governor asked him, saying, Art thou the king of the Jews? And Jesus said unto him, Thou sayest. And when he was accused of the chief priests and elders, he answered nothing. Then said Pilate unto him, Hearest thou not how many things they witness against thee? And he answered him to never a word; insomuch that the governor marvelled greatly. Now at that feast the governor was wont to release unto the people a prisoner, whom they would. And they had then a notable prisoner, called Barabbas. Therefore when they were gathered together, Pilate said unto them, Whom will ye that I release unto you? Barabbas, or Jesus which is called the Christ? For he knew that for envy they had delivered him. When he sat down on the judgment seat, his wife sent unto him, saying, Have thou nothing to do with that just man: for I have suffered many things this day in a dream because of him. But the chief priests and the elders persuaded the multitude that they should ask Barabbas, and destroy Jesus. The governor answered and said unto them, Why, what evil hath he done? But they cried out the more, saying, Let him be crucified. When Pilate saw that he could prevail nothing, but that rather a tumult was made, he took water, and washed his hands before the multitude, saying, I am innocent of the blood of this just person: see ye to it. Then answered all the people,

His blood be on us, and on our children. Then released he Barabbas unto them: and when he had scourged Jesus, he delivered him to be crucified. Then the soldiers of the governor took Jesus into the common hall, and gathered unto him the whole band of soldiers. And they stripped him, and put on him a scarlet robe. And when they had platted a crown of thorns, they put it upon his head, and a reed in his right hand: and they bowed the knee before him, and mocked him, saying, Hail, King of the Jews! And they spit upon him, and took the reed, and smote him on the head. And after they had mocked him, they took the robe off from him, and put his own raiment on him, and led him away to crucify him. And as they came out they found a man of Cyrene, Simon by the name: him they compelled to bear his cross. And when they were come unto a place called Golgotha, that is to say, a place of a skull, They gave him vinegar to drink mingled with gall: and when he had tasted thereof, he would not drink. And they crucified him, and parted his garments, casting lots: that it might be fulfilled which was spoken by the prophet, They parted my garments among them, y cast lots. And sitting down they watched him there; And set up over his head his accusation written, THIS IS JESUS THE KING OF THE JEWS. Then were there two thieves crucified with him, one on the right hand and another on the left. And they that passed by reviled him, wagging their heads, And saying, Thou that destroyest the temple, and buildest it in three days, save thyself. If thou be the Son of God, come down from the cross. Likewise also the chief priests mocking him, with the scribes and elders, said, He saved others; himself he cannot save. If he be the King of Israel, let him now come down from the cross, and we will believe him. He

trusted in God; let him deliver him now, if he will have him: for he said, I am the Son of God. The thieves also, which were crucified with him, cast the same in his teeth....

What a most horrifying description in full detail of the most brutal, and most unjust treatment of any man in human history: Somebody said: But this man... the prophet Isaiah declared of Jesus, that he was wounded for our transgressions, bruised for our iniquities, the chastisement of our peace was upon him! Someone else declared: He that knew no sin was made sin for us that we might become the righteousness of God in him! Somebody said: God was in Christ reconciling the world unto himself: But Matthew continued:

... Now from the sixth hour there was darkness over all the land unto the ninth hour. And about the ninth hour Jesus Cried with a loud voice, saying, Eli, Eli, lama sabachthani? that is to say, My God, my God, Why hast thou forsaken me?

This cry is the most agonizing cry – the cry of death – the cry of complete and absolute separation Almighty God! Sin, my friend separates us from God in any of its forms. God can not have any parts of sin! Jesus for the first time since the beginning when the Word was with God was now separated from God as a result of taking on the sins of the entire human race: Yet while you and I were sinners Christ died for us!

Caiaphas the high priest in a rage after Jesus would not answer him a word, demanded Jesus saying, I adjure thee by the living God, that thou tell us whether thou be the Christ, the Son of God! The Sanhedrin accused Jesus of blasphemy passing down a verdict of guilty of death.

Pilate the governor, said that he found no fault in Jesus, and attempted to set him free but the crowd chose Barabbas over Jesus demanding his death by crucifixion! Pilate washed his hands of the situation, yet his hands still yields the blood of Jesus on them. He delivered Jesus over to be crucified, even after finding no fault in him.

Judas Iscariot betrayed him with the kiss of death, all the other disciples left him and fled, Peter denied him three times on an oath and cursing: God forsook Jesus at the very split second of his death! That agonizing cry though, the cry which caused nature to be moved by God, the cry which still today this very moment in time can be heard around the entire not only the world but I believe the entire universe! It is the most agonizing cry…

Eli, Eli Lama Sabachthani? that is to say, My God, my God, Why hast thou forsaken me?

The prophet Isaiah cried, Who have believed our report? Matthew continued… … **Some of the that stood there, when they heard that, said, This man calleth for Elias. And straightway one of them ran, and took a spunge, and filled it with vinegar, and put it on a reed, and gave him to drink. The rest said, Let be, let us see whether Elias will come to save him. Jesus when he had cried again with a loud voice, yielded up the ghost. And, behold, the veil of the temple was rent in twain, from the top to the bottom; and the earth did quake, and the rocks rent;… Now when the centurion, and they that were with him, watching Jesus, saw the earthquake, and those things that were done, they feared greatly, saying, truly this was the Son of God…." (Matthew-27:1-51, 54 KJV.)**

CHAPTER SIX
EYEWITNESSES OF HIS MAJESTY

"... For we have not followed cunningly devised fables, when we made know unto you the power and coming of our Lord Jesus Christ, but were eyewitnesses of his majesty. For he received from God the father honour and glory, when there came such a voice to him from the excellent glory, This is my beloved Son, in whom I am well pleased. And this voice which came from heaven we heard, when we were with him in the holy mount. We have a more sure word of prophecy; whereunto ye do well that ye take heed, as unto a light that shineth in a dark place, until the day dawn, and the day star arise in your hearts: Knowing this first, that no prophecy of the scripture is of any private interpretation. For the prophecy came not in old time by the will of man: but holy men of God spake as they were moved by the Holy Ghost.

Peter was one of the twelve whom Jesus called, and Peter's occupation, was that of a fisherman, as were they all except Luke whom was a beloved physician and Matthew whom was a tax collector. These testified via documentation noted in the scriptures, and John was more detailed in my opinion then most when he authored his within the confinement of his first epistle wherein John writes according to the scriptures these words with great boldness: **"That which was from the beginning, which we have heard, which we have seen with our eyes, which we have looked upon, and our hands have handled, of the word of life; (For the life was manifested and we have seen it, and bear witness, and shew unto you that eternal life, which was with the Father, and was manifested unto us;) That which we have seen and heard declare we unto you, that ye also may have fellowship with us: and truly our fellowship is with the Father, and with his son Jesus Christ...." (1 John-1:1-3 KJV.)**

Another of the writers declared in his epistle to the Hebrew believers these very significant words:

"God, who at sundry times and in divers manners spake in times past unto the fathers by the prophets, hath in these last days spoken unto us by his Son, whom he hath appointed heir of all things, by whom also he made the worlds; Who being the brightness of his glory, and the express image of his person, and upholding all things by the word of his power, when he had by himself purged our sins, sat down on the right hand of the majesty on high; Being made so much better than the angels, as he hath by inheritance obtained a more excellent name than they. For unto which of the angels said he at any time, Thou art my Son, this day have I begotten thee? And again, I will be to him a Father, and he shall be to me a Son? And again, when he bringeth in the firstborn into the world, he saith, And let all the angels of God worship him. And of the angels he saith, Who maketh his angels spirits, and his ministers a flame of fire. But unto the Son he saith, Thy throne, O

God, is for ever and ever: a sceptre of righteousness is the sceptre of thy kingdom....." (Hebrews-1:1-8 KJV.)

Each of us whom the Lord calls must meet the Lord Jesus Christ as we travel this highway of what is known to us as life. God have a specific time and place for each of our conversions. Most times when God stop us in the midst of our own lustfulness of the world, we are in a very bad place with no other place in this world to turn. God doesn't violate our free will as we are free moral agents; nor can God create godly character within the spirit of our being without our allowing him – God will not go against our will but I have come to believe that Almighty God will override our will for his divine purpose through creating circumstances by his divine hand of providence: the prophet Jonah is a case in point; you know the story:

Apostle Peter put or said it another way according to (2 Peter-3:1-15 KJV) wherein the apostle writes these very significant words:

"This second epistle, beloved, I now write unto you; in both which I stir up your pure minds by way of remembrance: That ye be mindful of the words which were spoken before by the holy prophets, and of the commandments of us the apostles of the Lord and Savior: Knowing this first, that there shall come in the last days scoffers, walking after their own lusts, And saying, Where is the promise of his coming? for since the fathers fell asleep, all things continue as they were from the beginning of the creation. For this they willingly are ignorant of, that by the word of God the heavens were of old, and the earth standing out of the water, and in the water: Whereby the world that then was, being overflowed with water, perished: But the heavens and the earth, which are now, by the same word are kept in store, reserved unto fire against the day

of judgment and perdition of ungodly men. But, beloved, be not ignorant of this one thing, that one day is with the Lord as a thousand years, and a thousand years as one day. The Lord is not slack concerning his promise, as some me count slackness; but is longsuffering to us-ward. Not willing that any should perish, but that all should come to repentance. But the day of the Lord will come as a thief in the night; in the which the heavens shall pass away with a great noise, and the elements shall melt with fervent heat, the earth also and the works that are therein shall be burned up. Seeing then that all these things shall be dissolved. What manner of persons ought ye to be in all holy conversation and godliness, Looking for and hasting unto the coming of the day of the God, [Jesus Christ,] wherein the heavens being on fire shall be dissolved, and the elements shall melt with fervent heat? Nevertheless we, according to his promise, look for new heavens and a new earth, wherein dwelleth righteousness. Wherefore, beloved, seeing that ye look for such things, be diligent that ye may be found of him in peace, without spot, and blameless. And account that the longsuffering of our Lord is salvation; ..."

My friend, Jesus Christ made a promise that he is going to keep, nothing in heaven, in this earth, underneath this earth can alter that promise: Do you recall that promise of which Jesus promised, and Peter is referring?

"Let not your heart be troubled: Ye believe in God, believe also in me. In my Father's house are many mansions: if it were not so, I would have told you. I go to prepare a place for you. And if I go and prepare a place for you, I will come again, and receive you unto myself; that where I am, there ye may be also. And the

And whither I go ye know, and the way ye know…."
(John-14:1-4 KJV.)

Looking back again at the closing of chapter five, Matthew declared these vital words:

"…. Jesus, when he had cried again [Eli, Eli, Lama Sabachthani? that is to say, My God, my God, Why hast thou forsaken me?] **with a loud voice, yielded up the ghost.**

Jesus had drunk of the cup of sin and death and complete separation from God which he in the garden prayed that God would take from him but not his will but the Father's will be done: then Jesus Christ died! He had poured his soul [His physical life and its consciousness! Which life was in his blood!] Jesus was dead completely and absolutely dead. God Is taking me back within the Spirit of my mind as he is leading my mind in the writing of this book entitled, The Most Agonizing Cry – subtitled, Eli, Eli, Lama Sabchthani? I thought that I was lost in the book but God Almighty is never, ever, ever lost as God knows what he's doing and yes, my friend, I simply follow his leading: back to the burial and the resurrection of Jesus Christ after he was crucified. As Matthew continues with the details as these disciples were eyewitnesses of his majesty according to (Matthew-27:57-66 KJV) wherein Matthew declares:

… When the evening was come, there came a rich man of Arimathaea, named Joseph, whom also himself was Jesus' disciple: He went to Pilate, and begged the body of Jesus. Then Pilate commanded the body to be delivered. And when Joseph had taken the body, he wrapped it in a clean linen cloth, And laid it in his own new tomb, which he had hewn out in the rock: and he rolled a great stone to the door of the sepulchre, and departed. And there was Mary Magdalene, and the other Mary, sitting over against the sepulchre. Now the next day, that followed the day of the preparation, the

chief priests and the Pharisees came together unto Pilate, Saying, Sir, we remember that that deceiver said, while he was yet alive, After three days I will rise again. Command therefore that the sepulchre be made sure until the third day, lest his disciples come by night, and steal him away, and unto the people, He is risen from the dead: so the lest error shall be worse than the first. Pilate said unto them, Ye have a watch: go your way, make it as sure as you can. So they went, and made the sepulchre sure, sealing the stone, and setting a watch." "In the end of the Sabbath, as it began to dawn towards the first day of the week, came Mary Magdalene and the other Mary to see the sepulchre. And, Behold, there was a great earthquake: for the angel of the Lord ascended from heaven, and came and rolled back the stone from the door, and sat upon it. His countenance was like lightening, and his raiment white as snow: And for fear of him the keepers did shake, and became as dead men. And the angel answered and said unto the women, Fear not ye: for I know that ye seek Jesus, which was crucified. He is not here: for he is risen, as he said. Come, see the place where the Lord lay. And go quickly, and tell his disciples that he has risen from the dead; and, behold, he goeth before you into Galilee; there shall ye see him: lo, I have told you. And they departed quickly from the sepulchre with fear and great joy; and did run to bring his disciples word. And as they went to tell his disciples, behold, Jesus met them, saying, All hail, And they came and held him by the feet, and worshipped him. Then said Jesus unto them, Be not afraid: go tell my brethren that they go into Galilee, and there shall they see me. Now when they were going, behold, some of the watch came into the city, and shewed unto the chief priests all the things that were done. And when they were assembled with the elders, and had taken counsel, they gave large money unto the soldiers, Saying, Say ye, His disciples came by night, and stole him away while we slept. And if this comes to the governor's ears, we will persuade him, and secure you. So they took the money, and did as they were taught: and this saying is commonly reported among the Jews until this day. Then the eleven disciples went away into Galilee, into a mountain where Jesus had appointed them. And when they saw him, they worshiped him: but some doubted, And Jesus came and spake unto them, saying, All power is given unto me in heaven and in earth. Go ye therefore, and teach all nations, baptizing them in the name of the Father, and of the Son, and of the Holy Ghost: Teaching them to observe all things whatsoever I have commanded you: and, lo, I am with you always, even unto the end of the world...." (Matthew-28:1-20 KJV.)

Wow, what deep, deep details of which Matthew have documented in his gospel. Look at what Jesus went through for you and me, and not for us only but for the entire world. What a life and legacy our Lord and Savior left behind for us to know him even in a deeper sense than we used to. Matthew have brought us just a little closer to know our God.

Jesus Christ was brutally beaten, spit on, pierced in his side, marred worse than any man in the history of humanity even to this very second in time: But this man! Jesus, Jesus, Jesus! I can hear somebody saying within the spirit of my mind these words of vital significance:

".... For when we were yet without strength, in due time Christ died for the ungodly. For scarcely for a righteous man will one die: yet peradventure for a good man some would even dare to die. But God commanded his love

toward us, in that, while we were yet sinners, Christ died for us. Much more then, being now justified by his blood, we shall be saved from wrath through him. For if, when we were enemies, we were reconciled to God by the death of his Son, much more, being reconciled, we shall be saved by his life. And not only so, but we also joy in God through our Lord Jesus Christ, by whom we have now received the atonement...." (Romans-5:6-11 KJV.)

My friend, as my mother always said, Praise God for Jesus: She understood this very well that at her demise by means of stage four lung cancer she did not let it move her from her faith.

If Jesus Christ continues to tarry, we all will continue to die by some means unknown to us but well known to God Almighty: Will you be able to not be moved from your faith? Will you be able to say, I have fought a good fight, I have finished my course, I have kept the faith?

The day of our death will be the ultimate trying of our faith: that day will be THE day, will you my friend, be ready?

My friend, if you do not know Jesus in the pardon of your sins, now is the time for you to come to that decision: It is said that, If you confess with your mouth the Lord Jesus and believe in your heart that God raised him from the dead you shall be saved – understand that promise is instantly and that salvation is a life-long process: We are sealed by the Holy Spirit at the very instant we confess and believe, and that until the process is complete at the coming of our Lord and Savior and our God. He that believeth on the name of the Son of God have everlasting life: He that believeth not the Son shall not see life and the wrath of God abides on him! Do you believe?

CHAPTER SEVEN
CUT OFF OUT OF THE LAND OF THE LIVING

"… He was taken from prison and from judgment: and who shall declare his generation? for he was cut off out of the land of the living: for the transgression of my people was he stricken…." (Isaiah-53:8 KJV.)

Let me give you this verse from a parallel translation for a better understanding of it: I believe God that once you comprehend this verse in a much clearer translation that you too will then feel the most agonizing cry of Jesus while on the cross at the place called the skull:

"… He was led away after an unjust trial-but who even cared? Indeed, he was cut off from the land of the living; because of the rebellion of his own people he was wounded…." (NET Bible.)

When Jesus was challenged by the chief priests and the Pharisees as by whom authority he taught in the temple Jesus spoke to them in what is called parables: A parable according to the Merriam-Webster Dictionary is defined as follows: a simple story told to illustrate a moral truth.

John declared that Jesus was in the world and that the world was made by him, but the world knew him not and that he came unto his own and his own received him not: It was because of the rebellion against him by the Jews – his own flesh and blood people that he was murdered – cut off out of the land of the living. In (Matthew-21:33-46 KJV) is documented this parable of the wicked husbandmen: Listen carefully or you will miss it:

"... Hear another parable: There was a certain householder, which planted a vineyard, and hedged it round about, and digged a winepress in it, and built a tower, and let it out to husbandmen, and went into a far country: And when the time of the fruit drew near, he sent his servants to the husbandmen, that they might receive the fruits of it. And the husbandmen took his servants, and beat one, and killed another, and stoned another. Again, he sent other servants more than the first: and they did unto them likewise. But last of all he sent unto them his son, saying, They will reverence my son. But when the husbandmen saw the son, they said among themselves, This is the heir; come let us kill him, and let us seize on his inheritance. And they caught him, and cast him out of the vineyard, and slew him. When the Lord therefore of the vineyard cometh, What will he do unto those husbandmen? They say unto him, He will miserably destroy those wicked men, and will let out his vineyard unto other husbandmen, which shall render him the fruits in their seasons. Jesus said unto them, Did ye never read in the scriptures, The stone which the builders rejected, the same is become the head of the corner: this is the Lord's doing, and it's marvelous in our eyes? Therefore say I unto you, The kingdom of God shall be taken from you, and given to a nation bringing forth the fruits thereof. And whosoever fall on this stone shall be broken: but on whomsoever it shall fall, it will grind him to powder. And when the chief priest and Pharisees had heard his parables, they perceived that he spake of them. But

when they sought to lay hands on him, they feared the multitude, because they took him for a prophet."

Yes, my friend, I can hear the son of the householder in this parable crying out to his father to save him but his father was not there. Jesus cried out to his Father at the split seconds of his death, but God the Father had forsaken Jesus as God can have no parts of sin!

When I consider these things, it makes me feel so unworthy to be called a believer because it was my sins and your sins that Christ died for and not our only, but the sins of all humanity. God's will is that all me be saved and come to the knowledge of the truth.

In Paul's epistle to Timothy the apostle writes these words to his son in the faith:

"I exhort therefore, that, first of all, supplications, prayers, intersessions, and giving of thanks, be made for all men; for kings, and for all that are in authority; that we may live a quit and peaceable life in all godliness and honesty. For this is good and acceptable in the sight of God our Saviour; Who will have all me to be saved, and to come unto the knowledge of the truth. For there is one God, and one mediator between God and men, the man Christ Jesus; Who gave himself a ransom for all, to be testified in due time...." (1 Timothy-2:1-6 KJV.)

It is the divine ultimate will of the Almighty, that all men be saved and come to the knowledge of the truth which truth is in Christ Jesus our Lord. We as believers are to walk in wisdom towards those that are without because all men have not the faith.

We believers in and of ourselves are no better or no worse than those who are yet with faith, we are saved by the mercy and the grace of Almighty God. Jesus died for the sins of the entire world. For God so loved the world that he gave his only begotten Son, that WHOSOEVER believeth in him should not perish but have everlasting life. God di not send his Son into the world to condemn the world but that the world through him might be saved. He that believeth is not condemned, but he that believeth not is condemned already because he hath not believed in the name of the only begotten Son of God.

He that believeth in the Son of God have life but he that believeth not shall not see life and the wrath of God abides on him. And yes, my friend, this is the condemnation, John said; that Light have come into the world, and men loved darkness rather than light because their deeds were evil. Such men hate the Light and will not come to the Light because their deeds will be made known.

Do you know anyone in such a spiritual state? Is that someone you? Time is running out and the householder is about to return and when that day finally arrives in the earth men that believe not are without excuse!

Apostle John told of his revelation of the great white throne judgment, and of how he saw the dead both small and great stand before Almighty God in the great white throne judgment, and that the books were opened, and another book was opened, which was the book of life. And that each was judged by their works by the things that was written in the books. I would rather meet God now in peace than then in his ultimate wrath. This is your day to believe and be saved before the day of the Lord come upon this present evil world unknowingly to it! On that day, there will be no excuse as only the condemned will be standing at the great white throne judgment without excuse, condemned to eternal death, never to exist again as such will be cast into hell – the lake of fire and suffer the second death which death is eternal.

The most agonizing cry that is heard around this entire universe, was not just for believers, but for those who believe not: Jesus died for the sins of all humanity, which means for every single human being in the earth and under the earth in the grave. Only a fool says in the spirit of his mind – his heart; There is no God! There is a God and there is no excuse for the fool that do not believe! Watch this now or you will miss it: You better believe that God's wrath burns mightily against sin

"... For the wrath of God is revealed from heaven against all ungodliness and unrighteousness of men, who hold the truth in unrighteousness; Because that which may be known of God is manifest in them; for God hath shewed it unto them. For the invisible things of him from the creation of the world are clearly seen, being understood by the things that are made, even his eternal power and Godhead; so that they are without excuse. Because that, when they knew God, they glorified him not as God, neither were thankful; but became vain in their imaginations, and their foolish hearts were darkened. Professing themselves to be wise, they became fools, And changed the glory of uncorruptible God into an image made like to corruptible man, and to birds, and fourfooted beast, and creeping things. Wherefore God also gave them up to uncleanness through the lust of their own hearts, to dishonor their own bodies between themselves: Who changed the truth of God into a lie, and worshipped and served the creature more than the Creator, who is blessed for ever. Amen. For this cause God gave themo vile affections: for even their women did change the natural use into that which is against nature: And likewise also the men, leaving the natural use of the woman, burned in their lust one towards another; men

with men working that which is unseemly, and receiving within themselves that recompence of their error which was meet. And even as they did not like to retain God in their knowledge, God gave them over to a reprobate mind, to do those things which are not convenient; Being filled with all unrighteousness, fornication, wickedness, covetousness, maliciousness; full of envy, murder, debate, deceit, malignity, whisperers, Backbiters, haters of God, despiteful, proud, boasters, inventors of evil things, disobedient to parents, Without understanding, covenantbreakers, without natural affection, implacable, unmerciful: Who knowing the judgment of God, that they which commit such things are worthy of death, not only do the same, but have pleasure in them that do them." (Romans-1:18-32 KJV.)

Yes, my friend, men will be without excuse on the day of the final judgment. Jesus paid the price for mankind to look unto God and be saved: He poured his soul out unto death at Calvary even for those that believe not! That cry, the most agonizing cry; Eli, Eli, Lama Sabachthani? My God, my God, Why hast thou forsaken me? The prophet Isaiah asked the question: **"Who hath believed our report? ... Surely he hath born our grifes, and carried our sorrows: yet we did esteem him stricken, smitten of God, and afflicted. But he was wounded for our transgressions, he was bruised for our iniquities, the chastisement of our peace was upon him; and with his stripes we are healed. All we like sheep have gone astray; we have turned ever one to his own way; and the LORD hath laid on him the iniquities of us all..."**

CHAPTER EIGHT
THE TRAVAIL OF HIS SOUL

"... And he made his grave with the wicked, and with the rich in his death; because he had done no violence, neither was any deceit in his mouth. Yet it pleased the **LORD** to bruise him; he hath put him to grief: when thou shalt make his soul an offering for sin, he shall see his seed, he shall prolong his days, and the pleasure of the **LORD**, shall prosper in his hand. He shall see of the travail of his soul, and shall be satisfied: by his knowledge shall my righteous servant justify many; for he shall bear their iniquities. Therefore will I divide him a portion with the great, and he shall divide the spoil with the strong poured out his soul unto death: and he was numbered with the transgressors; and he bare the sins of many, and made intercession for the transgressors." (Isaiah-53:9-12 KJV.)

The physical life and its consciousness were in the "BLOOD" of Christ Jesus: It is the blood which Jesus poured out unto death and therein was the soul incorporated. Only the awesome Almighty God of the universe can completely understand this. God who created the human anatomy created the "SOUL" to be within the blood of every human being. This is beyond natural comprehension! It is only through the word of God, and the guidance of his Holy Spirit can this be even somewhat conceived within the spirit of even the spiritual mind: the psalmist declared that he was fearfully and wonderfully made.

Looking up the word travail in the Merriam Webster Dictionary; one definition is this: Agony, which is defined in the same as extreme pain in the mind or body. Jesus Christ literally suffered in his both mentally and physically even unto his death. However, spiritually Jesus Christ conquered death, in that, God the Father raised him from the dead: His flesh did not see corruption! Jesus scripture declares poured out his soul unto death – his precious blood was spilled into this earth and the earth as it did with Abel, opened her mouth and received it; yet the spill of that blood moved God to move nature itself and cause the vail in the temple to split in two. This was an earth shaking event in human history: It is the most agonizing cry which have resignated down through history even until this very second in time! Jesus Christ suffered beyond recognition as scripture declares that he was marred more than any man!

God when speaking with Moses during the days of Moses' lifetime regarding the sacredness of blood declared these words according to that which be documented in **(Leveticus-17:10-14 KJV:)**
"… And whatsoever man there be of the children of Israel, or of the stranger that sojourn among you, that eateth any manner of blood; I will even set my face against that soul that eateth blood, and will cut him off from among his people. For the life of the flesh is in the blood: and I have given it unto you upon the altar to make an atonement for your souls: for it is the BLOOD that maketh atonement for the SOUL. Therefore I said unto the children of Israel, No soul of

you shall eat blood, neither shall no stranger that sojourn among you eat blood. And whatsoever man ther be of the children of Israel, or of the stranger that sojourn among you, which hunteth and catcheth any beast or fowl that may be eaten; he shall even pour out the blood thereof, and cover it with dust. For it is the life of all flesh; the blood of it is for the life thereof: therefore I said unto the children of Israel, Ye shall eat the blood of no manner of flesh: for the life of all flesh is the blood thereof: whosoever eateth it shall be cut off...."

Yes, the blood of Christ Jesus is precious to the Almighty as it is not stained by sin and death: It is as pure as pure can be, and it STILL works!

Mark was another disciple and apostle which was an eyewitness of the crucifixion of our Lord and Savior Jesus Christ. We have witnessed the account of the event from the last supper to the death as is declared by Matthew; let me now take you back into the history of the biblical declaration of Mark's eyewitness of the same as I pick up the details as they be written in **(Mark-14:1-2. 10-72 KJV)** wherein Mark pens these vital details of this event as he witnessed with his own eyes:

"After two days was the feast of the Passover, and of unleavened bread: and the chief priests and the scribes sought how they might take him by craft, and put him to death. But they said, Not on the feast day, lest there be an uproar of the people. ... And Judas Iscariot, one of the twelve, went unto the chief priest, to betray him unto them. And when they heard it, they were glad, and promised to give him money. And he sought how he might conveniently betray him. And the first day of unleavened bread, when they killed the Passover, his disciples said unto him, Where wilt thou that we go

and prepare that thou mayest eat the Passover? And he sendeth forth two of his disciples, and saith unto them, Go ye into the city, and there shall meet you a man bearing a picture of water: follow him. And wheresoever he shall go in, say ye to the goodman of the house, The Master saith, Where is the guestchamber, where I shall eat the passover with my disciples? And he will shew you a large upper room, furnished and prepared; there make ready for us. And his disciples went forth, and came into the city, and found as he had said unto them: and they made ready the passover. And in the evening he cometh with the twelve. And as they sat and did eat, Jesus said, Verily, I say unto you, one of you which eateth with me shall betray me. And they began to be sorrowful, and to say unto him one by one, Is it I? and another said, is it I? And he answered and said unto them, It is one of the twelve, that dippeth with me in the dish. The Son of man indeed goeth, as it is written of him: but woe to that man by whom the Son of man is betrayed! good were it for that man if he had never been born. And as they did eat, Jesus took bread, and blessed, and break it, and gave to them, and said, Take, eat: this is my body. And he took the cup, and when he had given thanks, he gave it to them: and they all drank of it. And he said unto them, This is my blood of the new testament, which is shed for many. Verily I say unto you, I will drink no more of the fruit of the vine, until that day that I drink it new in the kingdom of God. And when they had song a hymn, they went out into the mount of Olives. And Jesus saith unto them, All ye shall be offended because of me this night: for it is written, I will smite the shepherd, and the sheep shall be scattered. But after that I am risen, I will go before you into Galilee. But Peter said unto him, Although all shall be offended, yet will not I. And Jesus saith unto him, Verily I say unto thee, That this day, even in this night, before the cock crow twice, thou shalt deny me thrice. But he spake the more vehemently, If I should die with thee, I will not deny thee in any wise. Likwise also said they all. And they came to a place which was named Gethsemane: and he saith to his disciples, Sit ye here, while I shall pray. And he taketh with him Peter and James and John, and began to be sore amazed, and to be very heavy; And saith unto them, My soul is exceeding sorrowful unto death: tarry ye here, and watch. And he went forward a little, and fell on the ground, and prayed that, if it were possible, the hour might pass from him. And he said, Abba, Father. All things are possible unto thee, take away this cup from me: nevertheless not what I will, but what thou wilt. And he cometh, and findeth them sleeping, and saith unto Peter, Simon, sleepest thou? couldest not thou watch one hour? Watch ye and pray, lest ye enter into temptation. The spirit truly is ready, but the flesh is weak. And again he went away, and prayed, and spake the same words. And when he returned, he found them asleep again, (for their eyes were heavy,) neither wist they what to answer him. And he cometh the third time, and saith unto them, Sleep on now, and take your rest: it is enough, the hour is come, behold, the Son of man is betrayed into the hands of sinners. Rise up, let us go; lo, he that betrayeth me is at hand. And immediately, while he yet spake, cometh Judas, one of the twelve, and with him a great multitude with swords and staves, from the chief priests and the scribes and the elders. And he that betrayed him had given them a token, saying, Whomsoever I shall kiss, that same is h; take him, and lead him away safely. And as soon as he was come, he goeth straightway unto him, and saith, Master, master; and kissed him. And they laid their hands on him, and took him. And one of them that stood by drew a sword, and smote a servant of the high priest, and cut off his ear. And Jesus answered and said unto them, Are ye come out, as against a thief, with swords and with staves to take me? I was daily with you in the temple teaching, and ye took me not: but the scriptures must be fulfilled. And they all forsook him and fled. And there followed him a certain young man, having a linen cloth cast about his naked body, and the young men laid hold on him: And he left the linen cloth, and fled from them naked. And they led Jesus away to the high priest: and with him were assembled all the chief priests and the elders and the scribes. And Peter followed him afar off, even into the palace of the high priest: and he sat with the servants, and warmed himself at the fire. And the chief priests and all the counsel sought for witness against Jesus to put him to death; and found none. For many bare false witness against him, but their witness agreed not together. And there arose certain, and bare false witness against him, saying, We heard him say, I will destroy this temple that is made with hands, and within three days I will build another made without hands. But neither so did their witness agree together. And the high priest stood up in the midst, and asked Jesus, saying, Answerest thou nothing? what is it which these witness against thee? But he held his peace, and answered nothing. Again the high priest asked him, and said unto him, Art thou the Christ, the Son of the Blessed? And Jesus said, I am: and ye shall see the Son of man sitting on the right hand of power, and coming in the clouds of heaven. Then the high priest rent his clothes, and saith, What need we any further witnesses? Ye have heard the blasphemy: what think ye? And they all condemned him to be guilty of death. And some began to spit on him, and to cover his face, and to buffet him, and to say unto him, Prophesy: and the servants did strike him with the palms of their hands. And as Peter was beneath in the palace, there cometh one of the maids of the high priest: And when she saw Peter warming himself, she looked upon him, and said, And thou also was with Jesus pf Nazareth. But he denied, saying, I know not, neither understand I what thou sayest. And he went out into the porch; and the cock crew. And a maid saw him again, and began to say to them that stood by, This is one of them: for thou art a Galilaean, and thy speech agreeth thereto. But he began to curse and to sware, saying, I know not this man of whom ye speak. And the second time the cock crew. And Peter called to mind the word that Jesus said unto him, Before the cock crow twice, thou shalt deny me thrice. And when he thought thereon, he wept."

"And straightway in the morning the chief priest held a consultation with the elders and scribes and the whole counsel, and bound Jesus, and carried him away, and delivered him to Pilate. And Pilate asked him, Art thou the King of the Jews? And he answering said unto him, Thou sayest it. And the chief priest accused him of many things: but he answered nothing. And Pilate asked him again, saying, Answerest thou nothing? behold how many things they witness against thee. But Jesus yet answered nothing; so that Pilate marveled. Now at that feast (Mark-15:1-38, 42-47 KJV) he released unto them one prisoner, whomsoever they desired, An, there was one named Barabbas, which lay bound with them that had made insurrection with him, who had committed murder in the insurrection. And the multitude crying aloud began to desire him to do as he had ever done unto them. But Pilate answered them, saying, Wilt ye that I release unto you the King of the Jews? For he knew that the chief priests had delivered him for envy. But the chief priests moved the people, that he should rather release Barabbas unto them. And Pilate answered and said again unto them, What wilt ye then that I should do unto him whom ye call the King of the Jews? And they cried out again, Crucify him. Then Pilate said unto them, Why, what evil hath he done? And they cried out the more exceedingly, Crucify him. And so Pilate, willing to content the people, released Barabbas unto them, and delivered Jesus, when he , had scourged him to be crucified. And the soldiers led him away into the hall, called Praetorium; and they called together the whole band. And they clothed him with purple, and platted a crown of thorns, and put it about his head and began to salute him, Hail, King of the Jews! And they smote him on the head with a reed, , and did spit upon him, and bowing their knees worshipped him. And when they had mocked him, they took off the purple from him, and put his own clothes on him, and led him out to crucify him. And they compel one Simon of Cyrenian who passed by, coming out of the country, the father of Alexander and Rufus, to bear his cross. And they bring him unto the place Golgotha, which is, being interpreted, The place of a skull. And they gave him to drink wine mingled with myrrh: but he received it not. And when they had crucified him, they parted his garments, castings lots upon them, what every man should take. And it was the third hour, and they crucified him. And the superscription of his accusation was written over, **THE KING OF THE JEWS.** And with him they crucify two thieves; the one on his right hand, and the other on his left. And the scripture was fulfilled, which saith, And he was numbered with the transgressors. And they that passed by railed on him, wagging their heads, and saying, Ah, thou that destroyest the temple, and buildest it in three days, Save thyself, and come down from the cross. Likewise the chief priests mocking said among themselves with the scribes, He saved others; himself he cannot save. Let Christ the King of Israel descend now from the cross, that we may see and believe. And they that were crucified with him reviled him. And when the sixth hour was come, there was darkness over the whole land until the ninth hour. And at the ninth hour Jesus cried with a loud voice, saying, Eloi, Eloi, lama sabachthani? which is, being interpreted, My God, my God, why hast thou forsaken me? And some of them that stood by, when they heard it, said, Behold, he calleth Elias. And one ran and filled a spunge full of vinegar, and put it on a reed, and gave him to drink, saying, Let alone; let us see whether Elias will come to take him down. And Jesus cried with a loud voice, and gave up the ghost. And the veil of the temple was rent in twain from the top to the bottom. And when the centurion, which stood over against him, saw that he so cried out, and gave up the ghost, he said, Truly this man was the Son of God. ... And now when even was come, because it was the preparation, that is, the day before the sabbath, Joseph of Arimathaea, an honourable counseller, which also waited for the kingdom of God, came, and went in boldly unto Pilate, and craved the body of Jesus. And Pilate marveled if he was already dead: and calling unto him the centurion, he asked him whether he had been any while dead. And when he knew it of the centurion, he gave the body to Joseph. And he brought fine linen, and took him down, and wrapped him in the linen, and laid him in a sepulchre which was hewn out of rock, and rolled a stone into the door of the sepulchre. And Mary Magdalene and Mary the mother of Joses beheld where he was laid. …And when the sabbath was past, (Mark-16:1-20 KJV) Mary Magdalene, and Mary the mother of James, and Salome, had bought sweet spices, that they might come and anoint him. And very early in the morning the first day of the week, they came unto the sepulchre at the rising of the sun. And they said among themselves, Who shall roll us away the stone from the door of the sepulchre? And when they looked, they saw that the stone was rolled away: for it was very great. And entering into the sepulchre, they saw a young man sitting on the right side, clothed in a long white garment; and they were affrighted. And he saith unto them, Be not affrighted: Ye seek Jesus of Nazareth, which was crucified: he is risen; he is not here: behold the place where they laid him. But go your way, tell his disciples and Peter that he goeth before you into Galilee: there shall ye see him, as he said unto you. And they went out quickly, and fled from the sepulchre; for they trembled and were amazed: neither said they any thing to any man, for they were afraid. Now when Jesus was risen early the first day of the week, he appeared first unto Mary Magdalene, out of whom he had cast seven devils. And she went and told them that had been with him, as they mourned and wept. And they, when they had heard that he was alive, and had been seen of her, believed not. After that he appeared in another form unto two of them, as they walked, and went into the country. And they went and told it unto the residue: neither believed they them. Afterward he appeared unto the eleven as they sat at meat, and upbraided them with their unbelief and hardness of heart, because they believed not them which had seen him after he was risen. And he said unto them, Go ye into all the world, and preach the gospel to every creature. He that believeth and is baptized shall be saved; but he that believeth not shall be damned. And these signs shall follow them that believe; In my name shall they cast out devils; they shall speak with new tongues; They shall take up serpents; and if they drink any deadly thing, it shall not hurt them; they shall lay hands on the sick, and they shall recover. So then after the Lord had spoken unto them, he was received up into heaven, and sat on the right hand of God. And they went forth, and preached every where, the Lord working with them, and confirming the word with signs following. Amen."

Glory to God that Mark have given us some more detailed documentation into the events leading up to the death of Jesus to that horrific cry: The most horrifying cry heard still around the world today: And though you and I was not there as was these disciples who were eye witnesses of these events, I tremble, and chills run through my spine as that horrible cry of death still rings in our ears today; all you have to do is allow the Lord God Almighty to speak to the spirit of your mind and that loud cry can and will be heard.

Mark pointed out to us several facts that Matthew did not: Mark pointed out that Jesus before Pilate professed to be the Son of God; that Barabbas was a murderer whom the crowd chose over Jesus to be set free and Jesus crucified: that it was in the Praetorium Hall where the soldiers clothed Jesus in royal clothing (purple) and mocked him as they kneeled and worshipped Jesus: It was also in this hall where they gambled on his clothing for his clothing (cast lots): He was crucified between two thieves as Jesus was numbered with these two thieves as a transgressor: Joseph that took the body of Jesus and entombed it in his own new tomb was a counsellor by profession; who went for the body of Jesus boldly before Pilate and Joseph also waited the kingdom of God: It was out of Mary Magdalene that Jesus cast seven devils: Went into deeper details of the resurrection and assension of Jesus Christ. Same details as Matthew but from the eyes and the ears of Mark: Their details do not contradict but collaborate one another.

Follow me on into chapter nine of this inspiring book entitled: The most agonizing cry; subtitled: Eli, Eli, lama sabachthani?

We will in chapter nine began with the eyewitness of the apostle and gospel writer Luke as we look into the spirit of his mind though Luke have been long dead, yet he speaks: You do not want to miss Luke's eyewitness as Luck was a physician by profession.

CHAPTER NINE
EYEWITNESS OF A BELOVED PHYSICIAN

"Now the feast of unleavened bread drew nigh, (Luke-22:1-23, 31-70 KJV) which is called the Passover. And the chief and scribes sought how they might kill him; for they feared the people. Then entered Satan into Judas surnamed Iscariot, being of the number of the twelve. And he went his way, and communed with the chief priests and captains, ow he might betray him unto them. And they were glad, and covenanted to give him money. And he promised, and sought opportunity to betray him unto them in the absence of the multitude. Then came the day of unleavened bread, when the Passover must be killed. And he sent Peter and John, saying, Go and prepare us the passover, that we may eat. And they said unto him, Where wilt thou that we prepare? And he said unto them, Behold, when ye are entered into the city, there shall a man meet you, bearing a picture of water; follow him into the house where he entereth in. And ye shall say unto the goodman of the house, , The Master saith unto thee, Where is the guestchamber, where I shall eat the passover with my disciples? And he shall shew you a large upper room furnished: there make ready. And they went, and found as he had said unto them: and they made ready the passover. And when the hour had come, he sat down, and the twelve apostles with him. And he said unto them, With desire I have desired to eat this passover with you before I suffer. For I say unto you, I will not anymore eat thereof, until it be fulfilled in the kingdom of God. And he took the cup, and gave thanks, and said, Take this, and divide it among yourselves: For I say unto you, I will not drink of the fruit of the vine, until the kingdom of God shall come. And he took bread, and gave thanks, and brake it, and gave unto them, saying, This is my body which is given for you: this do in remembrance of me. Likewise also the cup after supper, saying, the cup is the new testament in my blood, which is shed for you. But, behold, the hand of him that betrayeth me is with me on the table. And truly the Son of man goeth, as it was determined: but woe unto the man by whom he is betrayed! And they began to inquire among themselves, which of them it was that should do this thing. ... And the Lord said, Simon, Simon, behold, Satan hath desired to have you, that he may swift you as wheat: But I have prayed for thee, that thy faith fail not: and when thou art converted, strengthen thy brethren. And he said unto him, Lord, I am ready to go with thee, both into prison, and into death. And he said, I tell thee Peter, the cock shall not crow this day, before that thou shalt thrice deny that thou knowest me. And he said unto them,When I sent you without purse, and script, and shoes, lacked ye any thing? And they said, Nothing. Then said he unto them, But now, he that hath a purse, let him take it, and likewise his script: and he that hath no sword, let him sell his garment and buy one. For I say unto you, that this that is written, must yet be accomplished in me, And he was reckoned among the transgressors: for the things concerning me have an end. And they said, Lord, behold, here are two swords. And he said unto them, It is enough. And he came out, and went, as he was wont, to the mount of Olives; and his disciples also followed him. And when he was at the place, he said unto them, Pray that ye enter not into temptation. And he was withdrawn from them about a stone's cast, and kneeled down, and prayed. Saying, Father, If thou be willing, remove this cup from me: nevertheless not my will, but thine be done. and there appeared an angel unto him from heaven, strengthening him. And being in agony he prayed more earnestly: and his sweat were as it were great drops of blood falling down to the ground. And when he rose up from prayer, and was come to his disciples, he found them sleeping for sorrow, And said unto them, Why sleep ye? rise and pray, lest ye enter into temptation. And while he yet spake, behold a multitude, and he that was called Judas, one of the twelve, went before them, and drew near unto Jesus to kiss him. But Jesus said unto him, Judas, betrayeth the Son of man with a kiss? When they which were about him saw what would follow, they said unto him, Lord, shall we smite with the sword? And one of them smote the servant of the high priest, and cut off his right ear. And Jesus answered and said, Suffer ye thus far. And he touched his ear, and healed him. Then Jesus said unto the high priests, and captains of the temple, and the elders, which were come to him, Be ye come out, as against a thief, with swords and staves? When I was daily with you in the temple, ye stretched forth no hands against me: but this is your hour, and the power of darkness. Then took they him, and led him, and brought him into the high priest's house. And Peter followed afar off. And when they had kindled a fire in the midst of the hall, and were set down together, Peter sat down among them. But a certain maid beheld him as he sat by the fire, and earnestly looked upon him, and said, This man was also with him. And he denied him, saying, Woman, I know him not. And after a little while another saw him, and said, Thou art also of them. And Peter said, Man, I am not. And about the space of one hour after another confidently affirmed, saying, Of a truth this fellow was also with him: for he is a Galilaean. And Peter said man, I know not what thou sayest. And immediately, while he yet spake, the cock crew. And the Lord turned, and looked upon Peter. And Peter remembered the word of the Lord, how he had said unto him, Before the cock crow, thou shalt deny me thrice. And Peter went out, and wept bitterly. And the men that held Jesus mocked him, and smote him. And when they had blindfolded him, they struck him on the face, and asked him, saying, Prophesy, who is it that smote thee. And many other things blasphemously spake they against him. And as soon as it was day, the elders of the people and the chief priests and the scribes came together, and led him into their council, saying, Art thou the Christ? Tell us. And he said unto them, If I tell you, ye will not believe: And if I also ask you, ye will not answer me, nor let me go. Hereafter shall the Son of man sat on the right hand of the power of God. Then said they all, Art thou the Son of God? And he said unto them, Ye say that I am. And they said, What need we any further witness? For we ourselves have heard of his own mouth."

"And the whole multitude of them arose, and led him unto Pilate. And they began to accuse him,, saying, We found this fellow perverting the nation, and forbidding to give tribute to Caesar, saying that he himself is Christ a King. And Pilate asked him, saying, Art thou the King of the Jews? And he answered him and said, Thou sayest it. Then said Pilate to the chief priests and to the people, I find no fault in this man. And they were the more fierce, saying, He stirreth up the people, teaching throughout all Jewry, beginning from Galilee to this place. When Pilate heard of Galilee, he asked whether the man were a Galilaean. And as soon as he knew that he belonged unto Herod's jurisdiction, (Luke-23:1-56 KJV) he sent him to Herod, who himself also was at Jerusalem at that time. And when Herod saw Jesus, he was exceeding glad: for he was desirous to see him for of a long season, because he had heard many things of him; and he hoped to have seen some miracle done by him. Then he questioned with him in many words; but he answered him nothing. And the chief priests and scribes stood and vehemently accused him. And Herod with his men of war set him at nought, and mocked him, and arrayed him in a gorgeous robe, and sent him again to pilate. And the same day Pilate and Herod were made friends together: for before they were at enmity between themselves. And Pilate when he had called together the chief priests and the rulers and the people, Said unto them, Ye have brought this man unto me, as one that perverteth the people: and, behold, I, having examined him before you, have found no fault in this man touching those things whereof ye accuse him. No, nor yet Herod: for I sent you to him; and, lo, nothing worthy of death is done

unto him. I will therefore chastise him, and release
him. (For of necessity he must release one unto them
at the feast.) And they cried out all at once, saying,
Away with this man, and release unto us Barabbas:
(Who for a certain sedition made in the city, and for
murder, was cast into prison.) Pilate therefore, willing
to release Jesus, spake again to them. But they cried,
saying, Crucify him, crucify him. And he said unto
them the third time, Why, what evil hath he done? I
have found no cause of death in him: I will therefore
chastise him, and let him go. And they were instant
with loud voices, requiring that he might be crucified.
And the voices of them and of the chief priests
prevailed. And Pilate gave sentence that it should be
as they required. And he released unto them him that
for sedition and for murder was cast into prison,
whom they had desired; but he delivered Jesus to their
will. And as they led him away, they laid hold upon
one Simon, a Cyrenian, coming out of the country, and
on him they laid the cross, that he might bear it after
Jesus. And there followed him a great company of
people, and of women, which also bewailed and
lamented him. But Jesus turning unto them said,
Daughters of Jerusalem, weep not for me, but weep for
yourselves, and for your children. For, behold, the
days are coming, in the which they shall say, Blessed
are the barren, and the wombs that never bare, and the
paps which never gave suck. Then shall they begin to
say to the mountains, Fall on us, and to the hills, cover
us. For if they do these things in a green tree, what
shall be done in a dry? And there were also two other,
malefactors, one on the right hand, and the other on
the left. Then said Jesus, Father, forgive them; for they
know not what they do. And they parted his raiment,

and cast lots. And the people stood beholding. And the rulers also with them derided him, saying, He saved others; let him save himself, if he be Christ, the chosen of God. And the soldiers also mocked him, coming to him, and offering him vinegar, And saying, If thou be the king of the Jews, save thyself. And a superscription also was written over him, in letters of Greek, and Latin, and Hebrew, THIS IS THE KING OF THE JEWS. And one of the malefactors which were hanged, railed on him, saying, If thou be Christ, save thyself and us. But the other answering rebuked him, saying, Dost not thou fear God, seeing thou art in the same condemnation? And we indeed justly; for we receive the dur reward of our deeds: but this man hath done nothing amiss. And he said unto Jesus, Lord, remember me when thou comest into thy kingdom. And Jesus said unto him, Verily I say unto thee, To day shalt thou be with me in paradise. And it was about the sixth hour, and there was a darkness over all the earth until the ninth hour. And the sun was darkened, and the veil of the temple was rent in the midst. And when Jesus had cried with a loud voice, he said, Father, into thy hands I commend my spirit: and having said thus, he gave up the ghost. Mow when the centurion saw what was done, he glorified God, saying, Certainly this was a righteous man. And all the people that came together to that sight, beholding the things which were done, smote their breast, and returned. And all his acquaintance, and the women that followed him from Galilee, stood afar off, beholding these things. And behold, there was a man named Joseph, a counsellor; and he was a good man, and a just: (The same had not consented to the counsel and deed of them:) he was of Arimathaea, a city of the Jews: who also himself waited for the kingdom of God. This man went unto Pilate, and begged the body of Jesus. And he took it down, and wrapped it in linen, and laid it in a sepulchre that was hewn in stone, wherein man before never was laid. And that day was the preparation, and the sabbath drew on. And the women also, which came with him from Galilee, followed after, and beheld the sepulchre, and how his body was laid. And they returned, and prepared spices and ointments; and rested the sabbath day according to the commandment."

"Now upon the first day of the week, (Luke-24:1-12, 36-43, 50-53 KJV.) [For my lack of time please read Luke 24:13-25 at your own convenience.] very early in the morning, they came unto the sepulchre, bringing the spices which they had prepared, and certain others with them. And they entered in, and found not the body of the Lord Jesus. And it came to pass, as they were much perplexed thereabout, behold, two men stood by them in shining garments: And as they were afraid, and bowed down their faces to the earth, they said unto them, Why seek ye the living among the dead? He is not here, but is risen: remember how he spake unto you when he was yet in Galilee, Saying, The Son of man must be delivered into the hands of sinful men, and be crucified. And the third day rise again. And they remembered his words, and returned from the sepulchre, and told all these things unto the eleven, and to all the rest. It was Mary Magdalene, and Joanna, and Mary the mother of James, and other women that were with them, which told these things unto the apostles. And their words seemed to them as idle tales, and they believed them not. Then arose Peter, and ran unto the sepulchre; and stooping down, he beheld the linen clothes laid by themselves, and departed, wondering in himself at that which was come to pass. ... And as they thus spake, Jesus himself stood in the midst of them, and saith unto them, Peace be unto you. But they were terrified and affrighted, and supposed that they had seen a spirit. And he said unto them, Why are ye troubled? and why do thoughts arise in your hearts? Behold my hands and my feet, that it is I myself: handle me, and see; for a spirit hath not flesh and bones, as ye see me have. And when he had thus spoken, he shewed them his hands and his feet. And while they yet believed not for joy, and wondered, he said unto them, Have ye here any meat? And they gave him a piece of broiled fish, and of an honeycomb. And he took it, and did eat before them. ... And he led them out as far as to Bethany, and he lifted up his hands, and blessed them. And it came to pass, while he blessed them, he was parted from them, and carried up into heaven. And they worshipped them, and returned to Jerusalem with great joy: And were continually in the temple, praising and blessing God. Amen."

Glory be to God Almighty, Luke the beloved physician did indeed give us more detail than Matthew and Mark, yet the story of the events line up almost perfectly as each of these disciples told it as they saw it.

Luke focus was more on the two male factors crucified at each side of Jesus – the one mocked Jesus and the other rebuked the mocker by saying Don't you fear God being in the same condemnation? He went on to confess that those two deserved what they were going through but JESUS, didn't deserve that which he had to endure. Then he said to the Lord, I would imagine with his final breath; Lord, remember me when you come into your kingdom. Jesus said, Today you will be with me in paradise but of course Jesus was not specifically referring to that day because that day they went to the grave – Jesus was referring to a future time when the kingdom of God shall be established on this earth wherein dwelleth righteousness and wherein he will rule with a rod of iron as King of kings, and Lord of lords; Jesus will be KING over all this earth at which every knee shall bow in heaven and in the earth and under the earth and every tongue shall confess that JESUS CHRIST is LORD! What a day that will be? Glory, glory, glory!

Luke also declared that Jesus cried with a loud voice, saying, Father, forgive them for they know not what they do. Then Luke declared that Jesus said, Father, into thine hands I commend my spirt. What did Jesus mean? Certainly he wasn't making reference to his blood, as it was poured out as a sin offering into the earth, which opened her mouth to receive: He certainly wasn't referring to his soul, as it was incorporated within his blood; no, Jesus was making reference to the breath of life – spirit essence; that which God breathed into every human that comes into this world: It is that breath which returns back to God at the split second of any human's death.

Luke pointed out that after Jesus appeared to his disciples after his death, they though it was a spirit but Jesus corrected them by telling them that a spirit did not have flesh and bones as did he; then he allowed them to handle him so they could see that it was definitely Jesus. Then Jesus ascended after prayer out of the sight of the disciples into the heavens.

Now, my friends, Jesus Christ did it just for you, and me, and not for us only, but for the entire world. He gave his life or his soul – physical life and its consciousness as a ransom for many. Believe you this? come now into chapter ten and let us look within the spirit of the mind of John!

CHAPTER TEN
THE DISCIPLE WHOM JESUS LOVED

"... When Jesus therefore saw his mother, and the disciple standing by, whom he loved, he saith unto his mother, Woman, behold thy son! Then said he to the disciple, Behold thy mother! And from that hour that disciple took her unto his own home. ..." (John-19:26-27 KJV.)

Looking into the spirit of the mind of John, the disciple whom it be documented that Jesus loved. I believe the Spirit of Almighty God had me to begin this chapter with the mother of Jesus – Mary standing at the foot of his cross with John. I can not say exactly how Mary felt at the death of her child but I do know that it is something I pray you never, ever have to experience as I myself know the pain; the emotional effect; during and after the death of a child as I have had to walk in those shoes myself at the death of my eight day old daughter, Christina! I cannot even begin to express the trying of one's faith at such a time so I know that Mary had to have really been prayed up.

I think it vital to point out that even at his death, Jesus, looked down and saw the devastation of his mother and he committed her well being to his friend and the disciple whom he loved – John to care for his mother in his place:

What love he showed for his mother even at the very point of his death: He loved her unto death.

Our mothers will follow us through the darkest periods of our lives as God have instilled such a love within the spirit of a mother's mind which in most cases far exceeds that of a father as we find in these days and times that most homes are fatherless.

Mary, the mother of Jesus stood with her son in his darkest hour until his final cry: Eli, Eli, lama sabachthani?

It is really refreshing to recall this event forward within the spirit of the mind as the disciples reminds us of what Jesus Christ endured on our behalf. It is moving within the spirit, and sad at the same time.

At the last supper that Jesus shared with his disciples he instituted the Lord's Supper and told them as often as they partook of it they did remember his death until he come. The Israelites partook of it once every year: today Christians partake of it once a month in most churches. The wine is a representation of his blood shed for us, and the bread represents his body which was broken for us: We are to partake of the wine and the bread worthily or we bring damnation on ourselves dishonoring the death of our Lord Jesus Christ and scripture declare that because many have took and do take of this sacred ordinance "unworthily" many are sick among us and many have even died. We must examine ourselves before we partake of this sacred ordinance continually!

But as we continue to look into the final apostle's mind, he will take us on the final journey into the events which lead up to the crucifixion of Jesus Christ. Each of the four gospel writers were eyewitnesses of the account and told their experience in their own words, and John the disciple whom Jesus loved writes:

"… These things have I spoken unto you, that ye should not be offended. They shall put you out of the synagogues: yea, the time cometh, that whosoever killeth you will think that he doeth God service. And these things will they do unto you, because they have not known the Father, nor me. But these things have I told you, that when the time shall come, ye may remember that I told ye of them. And these things I said not unto you at the beginning, because I was with you. But now I go my way to him that sent me; …" (John-16:1-5 KJV.)

"When Jesus had spoken these words, he went forth with his disciples over the brook Cedron, where was a garden, into the which he entered, and his disciples. And Judas also, which betrayed him, knew the place: (John-18:1-40 KJV) for Jesus ofttimes resorted thither with his disciples. Judas then, having received a band of men and officers from the chief priests and Pharisees, cometh thither with lanterns and torches and weapons. Jesus therefore, knowing all things that should come upon him, went forth, and said unto them, Whom seek ye? They answered him, Jesus of Nazareth. Jesus saith unto them, I am he. And Judas also, which betrayed him, stood with them. As soon then as he had said unto them, I am he, they went backward, and fell to the ground. Then asked he them again, Whom seek ye? And they said, Jesus of Nazareth. Jesus answered, I have told you that I am he. If therefore ye seek me, let these go their way: That the saying might be fulfilled, which he spake, Of them which thou gavest me have I lost none. Then Simon Peter having a sword drew it, and smote the high priest's servant, and cut off his right ear. The servant's name was Malchus. Then said Jesus unto Peter, Put up thy sword into thy sheath: the cup which my Father hath given me, shall I not drink it? Then the band and the captain and officers of the Jews took Jesus, and bound him, And led him away to Annas first; for he was the father in law to Caiaphas, which was the high priest that same year. Now Caiaphas was he, which gave counsel to the Jews, that it was expedient that one man should die for the people. And Simon Peter followed Jesus, and so did another disciple, that disciple was known unto the high priest, and went in with Jesus into the palace of the high priest. But Peter stood at the door without. Then went out that other disciple, which was known unto the high priest, and spake unto her that kept the door, and brought in Peter. Then said the damsel that kept the door unto Peter, Art thou also one of this man's disciples? He saith, I am not. And the servants and officers stood there, who had made a fire of coals, for it was cold: and they warmed themselves: and Peter stood with them, and warmed himself. The high priest then asked Jesus of his disciples, and of his doctrine. Jesus answered him, I spake openly to the world; I ever taught in the synagogue, and in the temple, whither the Jews always resort; and in secret have I said nothing. Why askest thou me? ask them which heard me, what I have said unto them" behold, they know what I said. And when he had thus spoken, one of the officers which stood by struck Jesus with the palm of his hand, saying, Answerest thou the high priest so? Jesus answered him, If I have spoken evil, bear witness of the evil: but if well, why smitest thou me? Now Annas had sent him bound unto Caiaphas the high priest. And Simon stood and warmed himself. They said therefore unto him, Art not thou also one of his disciples? He denied it, and said, I am not. One of the servants of the high priest, being his kinsman whose ear Peter cut off, saith, Did not I see thee in the garden with him? Peter then denied again, and immediately the cock crew. Then led they Jesus from Caiaphas unto the hall of judgment; and it was early, and they themselves went not into the judgment hall, lest they should be defiled; but that they might eat the passover. Pilate then went out unto them, and said, What accusation bring ye against this man? They answered and said unto him, , If he were not a malefactor, we would not have delivered him up unto thee. Then said Pilate unto them, Take ye him, and judge him according to your law. The Jews therefore said unto him, It is not lawful for us to put any man to death: That the saying of Jesus might be fulfilled, which he spake, signifying what death he should die. Then Pilate entered into the judgment hall again, and called Jesus, and said unto him, Art thou the King of the Jews? Jesus answered him, Sayest thou this thing of thyself, or did others tell it thee of me? Pilate answered, Am I a Jew? Thine own nation and the chief priests have delivered thee unto me: What hast thou done? Jesus answered, My kingdom is not of this world: If my kingdom were of this world, then would my servants fight, that I should not be delivered to the Jews: but now is my kingdom not from hence. Pilate therefore said unto him, Art thou a king then? Jesus answered, Thou sayest that I am a king. To this end was I born, and for this cause came I into the world, that I should bear witness to the truth. Ever one that is of the truth heareth my voice. Pilate said unto him, What is truth? And when he had said this he went out again unto the Jews, and saith unto them, I find in

Barry S Ross

him no fault at all. But ye have a custom, that I should release unto you one at the passover: will you therefore that I release unto you the King of the Jews? Then cried they all again, saying, Not this man, but Barabbas. Now Barabbas was a robber."

"Then Pilate therefore took Jesus, (John-19:1-42 KJV) and scourged him. And the soldiers platted a crown of thorns, and put it on his head, and they put on him a purple robe, And said, Hail, King of the Jews! and they smote him with their hands. Pilate therefore went forth again, and saith unto them, Behold, I bring forth to you, that ye may know that I find no fault in him. Then came Jesus forth, wearing the crown of thorns, and the purple robe. And Pilate saith unto them, Behold, the man! When the chief priests therefore and officers saw him, they cried out, saying, Crucify him, crucify him. Pilate saith unto them, Take ye him, and crucify him. for I find no fault in him. The Jews answered him, We have a law, and by our law he ought to die, because he made himself the Son of God. When Pilate therefore heard that saying, he brought Jesus forth, and sat down in the judgment seat in a place that is called the Pavement, but in Hebrew, Gabbatha. And it was the preparation of the passover, and about the sixth hour: and he saith unto the Jews, Behold your King! But they cried out, Away with him, away with him, crucify him. Pilate saith unto them, Shall I crucify your King? The chief priests answered, We have no King but Caesar. Then he delivered him therefore unto them to be crucified. And they took Jesus, and led him away. And he bearing his cross went forth into a place called the place of a skull, which is called int the Hebrew Golgotha: Where they crucified him, and two other with him, on either side one, and Jesus in the midst. And Pilate wrote a title, and put it on the cross. And the writing was, JESUS OF NAZARETH THE KING OF THE JEWS. This title then read many of the Jews: for the place where Jesus was crucified was nigh to the city: and it was written in Hebrew, and Greek, and Latin. Then said the chief priests of the Jews to Pilate, Write not the King of the Jews; but that he said, I am King of the Jews. Pilate answered, What I have written I have written. Then the soldiers, when they had crucified Jesus, took his garments, and made four parts, to every soldier a part; and also his coat: now the coat was without seam, woven from the top throughout. They said therefore among themselves, Let us not rend it, but cast lots for it, whose it shall be: that the scripture might be fulfilled, which saith, They parted my raiment among them, and for my vesture they did cast lots. These things therefore the soldiers did. Now there stood by the cross of Jesus is mother, and his mother's sister, Mary the wife of Cleophas, and Mary Magdalene. When Jesus therefore saw his mother, and the disciple standing by, whom he loved, he saith unto his mother, Woman, behold thy son! Then said he to the disciple, Behold thy mother. And from that hour that disciple took her unto his own home. After this, Jesus knowing that all things were now accomplished, that the scriptures might be fulfilled, saith, I thirst. Now there was set a vessel full of vinegar: and they filled a spunge with vinegar, and put it upon hyssop, and put it to his mouth. When Jesus therefore had received the vinegar, he said, It is finished: and he bowed his head, and gave up the ghost. The Jews therefore, because it was the preparation, that the bodies should not remain upon the cross on the sabbath day, (for that sabbath day was a high day,) besought Pilate that their legs might be broken, and that they might be taken away. Then came the soldiers, and brake the legs of the first, and of the other which was crucified with him. But when they came to Jesus, and saw that he was dead already, they brake not his legs. But one of the soldiers with a spear pierced his side, and forthwith came there out blood and water. And he that saw it bare record, and his record is true: and he knoweth that he saith true, that ye might believe. For these things were done, , that the scripture should be fulfilled, A bone of him shall not be broken. And again another scripture saith, They shall look on him whom they have pierced. And after this Joseph of Arimathaea, being a disciple of Jesus, but secretly for fear of the Jews besought Pilate that he might take away the body of Jesus: and Pilate gave him leave. He came therefore, and took the body of Jesus. And there came also Nicodemus, which at the first came to Jesus by night, and brought a mixture of myrrh and aloes, about a hundred pound weight. Then took they the body of Jesus, and wound it in linen clothes with the spices, as the manner of the Jews is to bury. Now in the place where he was crucified there was a garden, and in the garden a new sepulchre, wherein was never man yet laid. There laid they Jesus therefore because of the Jews' preparation day, for the sepulchre was nigh at hand."

"The first day of the week (John-20:1-29 KJV) cometh Mary Magdalene early, when it was yet dark, unto the sepulchre, and seeth the stone taken away from the sepulchre. Then she runneth, and cometh to Simon Peter, and to the other disciple, whom Jesus loved, and saith unto them, They have taken away the Lord out of the sepulchre, and we know not where they have laid him. Peter therefore went forth, and that other disciple, and came to the sepulchre. So they ran both together: and the other disciple did outrun Peter, and came first to the sepulchre. And he stooping down, and looking in, saw the linen clothes lying; yet went he not in. Then cometh Simon Peter following him, and went into the sepulchre, and seeth the linen clothes lie. And the napkin, that was about his head, not lying with the linen clothes, but wrapped together in a place by itself. Then went in also that other disciple, which came first to the sepulchre, and he saw, and believed. For as yet they knew not the scripture, that he must rise again from the dead. Then the disciples went away again unto their own home. But Mary stood without at the sepulchre weeping: and as she wept, she stooped down, and looked into the sepulchre, And seth two angels in white sitting, the one at the head, and the other at the feet, where the body of Jesus had lain. And they say unto her, Woman, why weepest thou? She saith unto them, Because they have taken away my Lord, and I know not where they have laid him. And when she had thus said, she turned herself back, and saw Jesus standing, and knew not that it was Jesus. Jesus saith unto her, Woman, why weepest thou? whom sleekest thou? She, supposing him to be the gardener, saith unto him, Sir, If thou hath borne him hence, tell me where thou hast laid him, and I will take him away. Jesus saith unto her, Mary. She turned herself, and saith unto him, Rabboni; which is to say, Master. Jesus saith unto her, Touch me not, for I am not yet ascended unto my Father: but go to my brethren, and say unto them, I ascend unto my Father, and your Father; and to my

God, and your God. Mary Magdalene came and told the disciples that she had seen the Lord, and that he had spoken these things unto her. Then the same day at even, being the first day of the week, when the doors were shut where the disciples were assembled for fear of the Jews, came Jesus and stood in the midst, and saith unto them, Peace be unto you. And when he had so said, he shewed unto them his hands and his side. Then were the disciples glad, when they saw the Lord. Then said Jesus to them again, Peace be unto you: As my Father hath sent me, even so send I you. And when he had said this, he breathed on them, and saith unto them, Receive ye, the Holy Ghost: Whosoever sins ye remit, they are remitted unto them; and whose soever sin ye retain, they are retained. But Thomas, one of the twelve, called Didymus, was not with them when Jesus came. The other disciples therefore said unto him, We have seen the Lord. But he said unto them, Except I shall see in his hands the print of the nails, and put my finger into the print of the nails, and thrust my hand into his side, I will not believe. After eight days again his disciples was within, and Thomas with them: then came Jesus, the doors being shut, and stood in the midst, and said, Peace be unto you. Then saith he to Thomas, Reach hither thy finger, and behold my hands; and reach hither thy hand, and thrust it into my side: and be not faithless, but believing. And Thomas answered and said unto him, My Lord and my God. Jesus saith unto him, Thomas, because thou hast seen me, thou hast believed: blessed are they that have not seen, and yet have believe. ..."

John certainly put forth more details in the betrayal, crucifixion, and the death of Jesus Christ: The most significant in my own personal opinion is the statement Thomas declared after he physically handled the prints of the nails in Jesus' hands, and the thrust of his hand into his side and was so awed by it that Thomas confessed; My Lord and my God! Can you even attempt to imagine you in the place of Thomas? Do you believe?

Jesus said to Thomas, be not faithless but believing: Thomas believed after he handled Jesus' resurrected body after physical proof that it was indeed Jesus Christ. Jesus said he believed only because he had seen Jesus after death, alive and well but BLESSED are those of us that have not seen and yet we believe! Somebody just said in the spirit of my mind, that SOME men have not faith! Listening again to the Spirit of the Almighty, I can here the old prophet Isaiah in the fifty-fifth chapter of the book he authored saying these very significant words again this very moment within the spirit of my mind:

"Who has believed our message? To whom has the LORD revealed his powerful arm? My servant grew up in the LORD'S presence like a tender green shoot, like a root in dry ground. There was nothing beautiful or majestic about his appearance, nothing to attract us to him. He was despised and rejected – a man of sorrows, acquainted with deepest grief. We turned our backs on him and looked the other way. He was despised, and we did not care. Yet it was our weaknesses he carried; it was our sorrows that weighed him down. And we thought his troubles were a punishment from God, a punishment for his own sins. But he was pierced for our rebellion, crushed for our sins. He was beaten so we could be whole. He was whipped so we could be healed. All of us, like sheep, have strayed away. We have left God's paths to follow our own. Yet the LORD laid on him the sins of us all.

He was oppressed and treated harshly, yet he never said a word. He was led like a lamb to the slaughter. And as a sheep is silent before the shearers, he did not open his mouth. Unjustly condemned, he was led away. No one cared that he died without descendants, that his life was cut short in midstream. But he was struck down for the rebellion of my people. He had done no wrong and had never deceived anyone. But he was bruised like a criminal; he was put in a rich man's grave. But it was the LORD'S good plan to crush him and cause him grief. Yet when his life (SOUL) is made an offering for sin, he will have many descendants. He will enjoy a long life, and the LORD'S good plan will prosper in his hand. When he sees all that is accomplished by his anguish, he will be satisfied. And because of his experience, my righteous servant will make it possible for many to be counted righteous, for he will bear all their sins. I will give him the honors of a victorious soldier, because he exposed himself to death. He was counted among the rebels. He bore the sins of many and interceded for rebels." (NLT – New Living Translation.)

Praise God for Jesus my friends, as this inspiring book comes to its closing. Jesus Christ paid it all, and he poured out his physical life and its consciousness – his soul unto death just for you and me. Jesus Christ was GOD in the flesh. Thomas declared of him, My Lord and my God. Apostle Paul declared, Great is the mystery of godliness: "… And without controversy great is the mystery of godliness: God was manifest in the flesh, justified in the Spirit, seen of angels, preached unto the Gentiles, believed on in the world, received up into glory." (1 Timothy-3:16 KJV.)

The most agonizing cry: Eli, Eli, lama sabachthani?

ABOUT THE AUTHOR

Visit amazon.com/Barry-Ross/e/B009KVCAVM

Made in the USA
Middletown, DE
26 November 2022

16054362R00061